Collecting Monster Toys

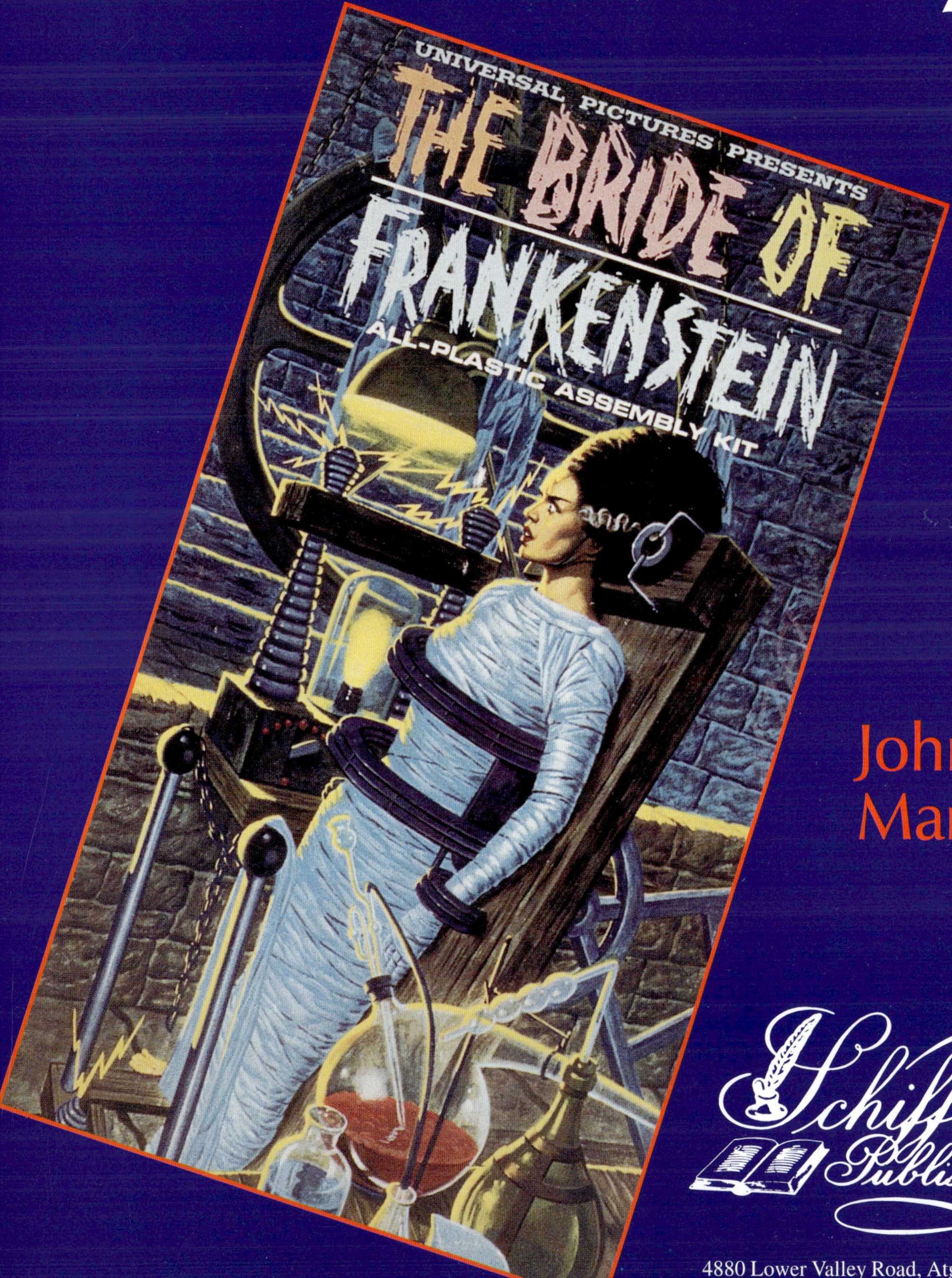

John Marshall

Schiffer Publishing Ltd
4880 Lower Valley Road, Atglen, PA 19310 USA

COPYRIGHT NOTICE

The monsters on which the merchandise shown in this book is based, as well as related characters, symbols, and logos, are all trademarked and/or copyrighted properties.

None of the copyright/trademark holders in any way authorized this book, nor furnished or approved any of the information contained therein. This book is for the information, use, and entertainment of collectors. This book in no way attempts to infringe on any copyright or trademark.

Copyright © 1999 by John Marshall
Library of Congress Catalog Card Number: 99-62484

All rights reserved. No part of this work may be reproduced or used in any form or by any means—graphic, electronic, or mechanical, including photocopying or information storage and retrieval systems—without written permission from the copyright holder.

"Schiffer," "Schiffer Publishing Ltd. & Design," and the "Design of pen and ink well" are registered trademarks of Schiffer Publishing Ltd.

Designed by "Sue"
Type set in Zaph Humanst Dm BT heading font/text font Humanst521 BT

ISBN: 0-7643-0923-4
Printed in China
1 2 3 4

Published by Schiffer Publishing Ltd.
4880 Lower Valley Road
Atglen, PA 19310
Phone: (610) 593-1777; Fax: (610) 593-2002
E-mail: Schifferbk@aol.com
Please visit our web site catalog at
www.schifferbooks.com or write for a free catalog.
This book may be purchased from the publisher.
Please include $3.95 for shipping.

In Europe, Schiffer books are distributed by
Bushwood Books
6 Marksbury Rd.
Kew Gardens
Surrey TW9 4JF England
Phone: 44 (0)181 392-8585; Fax: 44 (0)181 392-9876
E-mail: Bushwd@aol.com

Please try your bookstore first.

We are interested in hearing from authors
with book ideas on related subjects.

CONTENTS

ACKNOWLEDGMENTS 4

INTRODUCTION 5
HOW TO USE THIS BOOK 6

Chapter 1. UNIVERSAL MONSTERS 10
Chapter 2. CLASSIC MONSTERS OF MOVIES AND TV 50
Chapter 3. JAPANESE MOVIE MONSTERS 71
Chapter 4. JAPANESE TV MONSTERS 97
Chapter 5. MONSTERS UNLEASHED! 125
Chapter 6. MODERN MONSTERS 148

BIBLIOGRAPHY 160

ACKNOWLEDGEMENTS

Monster toys are popular and widespread and I needed plenty of help to pull together such a wide-ranging sampling of toys for you. Also, I consulted with many knowledgeable people for prices and such.

Scott Talis, who has contributed his knowledge and store stock to all of my previous books, was all too happy to help out once again. His extensive stock of super hero toys, monster toys, and character collectibles of all kinds can be seen at his store Play With This in the Pennsauken Mart, Pennsauken NJ 08110. (609) 486-4556.

Jim Adezio, proprietor of Toyrareum Collectible Toys, returns to astound us with rarities from his shop. See them live at 1101 Asbury Avenue, Ocean City, NJ 08226. (609) 391-0480.

Tim Welsh, a toy dealer who provided info on Captain Action for *Action Figures of the 1960s*, is here in full force this time, providing lots of the items you see in these pages. He deals in all kinds of cool character collectibles and can be emailed at actiondr@pics.com or phoned at (609) 735-9393. His official website is www.timmystoydungeon.com, and his mailing address is P.O. Box 24, Browns Mills NJ 08015.

Dave Clarke, my old friend whom I've often referred to as "Dave from Columbus Flea Market," pitched in a few items from his recently-inaugurated store, Kollector's Choice. It's located in Columbus Farmers Market, Columbus NJ (609) 261-2555.

Paul Levitt, the FX Channel's "Japanese Monster Maven" and chemist extraordinaire, provided his entire collection of monster toys, which included both Japanese rarities and the best in Universal Monsters collectibles. I'm proud to have his world-famous collection appearing exclusively in my book.

Our chum, the oft-quoted Nick Delliponti, was especially helpful with the "Modern Monsters" chapter. Our friend Sue Holmes, who has always wanted to contribute to one of my books, saw her dream come true at last in this one. Another first-timer, Aaron Kessler, pitched in some Dracula items from his enormous collection of bat-related paraphernalia. Fred Mahn didn't loan out anything, but why leave him out?

Special thanks go to my pal, the angelic TV sensation Myrka Dellanos. Her Spanish-language newsmagazine show *PRIMER IMPACTO* has the distinction of being the first international program to feature one of my books—albeit accidentally. Myrka had her copy of *Action Figures of the 1980s* lying on her desk when a behind-the-scenes segment was being filmed for "Take Your Daughter to Work Day" in 1998. And there was the 1980s book, plainly visible ... well, to anyone who knew what it looked like. Hey, I'll take what I can get, all right?

I really must give special thanks to Jeff Snyder, my editor (and photographer) at Schiffer Publishing. He is without a doubt the main reason that I continue to crank out toy books year after year, so I guess having me around the office a couple of times a month is his reward as well as his punishment.

I'd also like to extend my gratitude to Peter Schiffer, who has never turned down one of my proposals, and to all the wonderful hardworking people at Schiffer who have made the books (and the job opportunities and perks spun off from the books) so much fun to do.

As always, it can't hurt to thank God for my writing abilities, and the sense to use my powers for good and never evil. Well, (all together now) almost never!

This book is dedicated, as all my books are, to my sainted mother Janice Marshall, and my father, John Marshall Jr.—and to all the parents who let their kids watch *Chiller Theater*—even though it was so scary.

INTRODUCTION

When I was a boy, I lived in the New Jersey suburbs near Philadelphia, and we had a horror host on Channel 17, The Great Entertainer, named Dr. Shock. The good doctor was actually a close copy of America's most famous horror host, Zacherle, who is best known to New York monster movie fans. But we kids from "da Delaware Valley" didn't care. We just liked Dr. Shock, that's all.

The doctor would introduce Saturday afternoon broadcasts of monster movies and appear in skits that would pop up during the running time of the film, usually coming out of a commercial break or heading into one (much like the skits that are presented on *Mystery Science Theater 3000*). He would perform brain operations on cauliflowers, attempt to reanimate stagehands wearing Frankenstein masks, satirize our favorite local news personalities like Marc Howard and Jim O'Brien with "Hack-shun News", or do whatever he thought would hold a kid's attention.

But the truth was, of course, that as much as we enjoyed his antics, we didn't need Dr. Shock to convince us to watch those horror movies. We would have watched them anyway.

There is nothing like a monster movie to transport you away from reality for a few precious hours. Monster movies create for themselves an entire world, complete with its own laws and rules (silver bullets for werewolves, crosses for vampires!). Kids would huddle in tree houses or basements discussing the rules in order to keep them straight. Best of all, such arcane knowledge was beyond the understanding of parents, and that made it essential to any kid. Actually, the best illustration of this principle comes FROM a monster movie. In the wonderful 1980s movie *The Monster Squad*, a young boy's mother, trying to take an interest, says, "Dr. Van Helsing, he's the one who fights Godzilla, right?" Well, she tried. Grown-ups just never quite got it.

Plus, when kids got together to debate monster lore, they could compare notes on films they'd seen. Since this was in the days before VCRs, the best resource you had for a film you hadn't seen was the kid from down the street. "Yeah, they made a THIRD one, called *The Creature Walks Among Us*, where they give the Creature lungs!" And we would respond, "Really? What does he look like?" And the kid would say, with a little disappointment, "Well, he looks too much like Frankenstein, 'cause now he's wearing a shirt and his head isn't as scaly." But we all, still, wanted to see that movie.

The special attraction that kids have to monsters is easy to explain. A kid feels awkward and out of control of his environment (like Frankenstein or King Kong). He yearns for secret powers that will give him the ability to dominate or overpower the grownups (like Dracula or the Wolf Man). He often wishes he could just step on anybody who crosses him (like Godzilla or Frank Sinatra).

And that is why toys and the various other kid accouterments that feature monsters have always been incredibly popular. Amazingly enough, it took literally decades for toy manufacturers to catch on to this. Monster movies had been a major genre since the early 1930s, but it was thirty years before Marx and Aurora took their first tentative steps at releasing Frankenstein toys. The reason it finally happened was that one-eyed monster, "teevee." Many of the older films had been released to TV syndication in the late 1950s, so that all of these monsters were now the weekly companions of kids across the nation.

The real boom in monster merchandising came in the early 1960s, when Aurora decided to take a chance on releasing a model kit of Frankenstein's monster. Sales went absolutely through the roof, with the Aurora factory working overtime to produce kits.

Very rapidly, monster merchandising exploded with all manner of games, puzzles, and school supplies bearing the likenesses of the Universal Studios monsters like Frankenstein, Dracula, the Wolf Man, and the Mummy, plus that relatively late arrival—the Creature from the Black Lagoon. Other popular monsters, such as King Kong and Godzilla, got their own models and board games. Kong got a boost (and extra merchandising) from an animated cartoon show produced by Rankin-Bass in the early 1960s.

Kids are a fickle bunch, and by the mid-sixties monsters had been supplanted by the craze for spies (especially James Bond) and super heroes (especially Batman).

But in the 1970s, merchandising for kids hit a new high, and monsters were not forgotten. *The Monster Squad* was an action/comedy Saturday morning TV show that brought Dracula, Frankenstein, and the Wolf Man together to battle super villains. Godzilla got his own cartoon show in 1977, and Japanese heroes like Ultraman were giving kids a steady diet of giant Japanese monsters on a daily basis in syndication.

From that point on, the famous monsters of filmland were always having some kind of toy made in their likenesses, by somebody, somewhere. In 1991, for the 60th anniversary of Universal's Dracula and Frankenstein movies, Universal Studios began a licensing juggernaut that continues to this day, featuring some of the best monster items ever (like the Motionettes) and some of the worst (like the cheap bendies from Just Toys).

Japanese monster toys are also far more prevalent today, with dealers specializing in expensive imports that are actively gobbled up by collectors of all ages. When Trendmasters acquired the license to produce Godzilla toys for the American mass market, Japanese-issued Godzilla toys were embargoed and their values have soared. A Godzilla or Baragon or Rodan you could buy in a Japanese-owned store for $15-20 five years ago can be worth five to ten times that much today. The very same deluxe boxed Biollante figure that I hesitated to pay $50 for in 1993, people happily shell out $300-400 for now.

But that just goes to prove the enduring popularity of monsters. And not just movie monsters, either. An incredible monster menagerie has sprung up from all manner of movies and TV shows. Also, many modern monsters manifest from the minds of marketers specifically to be sold as toys, like Hasbro's Inhumanoids action figure line.

Thanks to cable, home video, and DVD, new generations of kids continue to discover all the classic monsters from movies and TV.

I think Dr. Shock would be proud.

John Marshall
Spring 1999

The Famous Monsters of Filmland official button, with a ghoulish Lon Chaney as Eric, the Phantom of the Horropera! $20-25. *Courtesy of Nick Delliponti.*

HOW TO USE THIS BOOK

It doesn't take the genius of Dr. Frankenstein to figure out that this book is divided into chapters based on groups of related monsters.

Rather than include a price guide covering all monster toys ever made, which could never be accurate anyway, I have decided to do the book as a pictorial, and include a substantial number of interesting collectibles related to each character. If a specific item you have isn't included, you can extrapolate the value from similar items that are presented here.

THE CAPTION PRICES

Each photo usually includes two price ranges for the item(s) in the photo. These refer to the amount you could expect to fork over to own such an item yourself.

THE "LOOSE" VALUE: Pricing of loose items is always based on that item's condition. "Loose" means "not in the package it came in." In brand-new shape, the value would be on the higher end. In used but serviceable shape, the lower end. The same item in worse shape, with broken or missing parts, could go for half as much as the low-end price or even less. That's why, as I always say, the mantra for the value of any collectible is "Condition, completeness, condition, completeness..."

THE "MINT IN PACKAGE" (MIP) VALUE: This refers to what the item is worth complete, in its original packaging (preferably unopened). This too has a range, because the condition of the package and whether the toy has ever been removed from it are major factors that separate the low-end price from the high-end price.

ITEMS WITH ONE PRICE RANGE: Some items have only one price range. Things like puzzles are basically inseparable from their packages. Other items are equally common loose or in the package, so only one price is necessary. In those cases, the low end on the price range is for the loose price and the high end on the price range is the mint in package price.

It is always smart to remember that price ranges only serve as a general guideline. When shopping for collectibles at antique shows, collector shops, flea markets and yard sales, always remember that prices vary from region to region, and that condition is everything. If I say a Mego 8" Wolf Man doll ranges from $60-75 loose, and you see one that is missing its boots and has a torn shirt, that does NOT mean it is worth $60. (Actually it isn't worth much of anything, except for parts.)

WHO'S INCLUDED, WHO ISN'T

The focus of this book is on the classic monsters who were heavily merchandised in the 1960s, 1970s and 1980s, who continue to be popular in the 1990s. There is also substantial coverage of recent inventions, like Freddy, whose impact on the toy world is undeniable.

The definition of a monster, for this book, is an inhuman creature of evil nature or intent, a prehistoric throwback aside from an ordinary dinosaur, a livingly-challenged individual (like Dracula), or all of the above. Not all evil or destructive characters are monsters, so, for instance, toys of your boss are not included.

WHAT'S INCLUDED, WHAT ISN'T

It isn't possible to fit all the monster toys ever made into one book. To list prices for toys not pictured is risky. Unlike action figures, which can be researched according to their interrelated product lines, monster toys have been manufactured in dozens of countries by hundreds of different companies over the course of decades. Therefore, toys that have not been encountered and photographed are not listed. All too often, price guides turn up in books and magazines that have cryptic listings like, "Dracula fangs, 1962, $29." How would you recognize them if you saw them? Is there more than one kind? Personally, I find listings like those worse than useless.

What constitutes a monster toy? It's simple—a monster toy is anything you can associate with being a kid, because nostalgia is what my books are all about. Thus, things like lunch boxes, technically not toys, are included. I have also included a few standout examples of modern collectibles aimed at the adult buyer, for their "ooh" and "aah" appeal. But I didn't overly concern myself with these items for two reasons. One, they were manufactured to be collectibles (not toys) and two, the values of "trendy" items like these are best covered by the seemingly endless numbers of collectibles magazines available at any news stand. Their values can change up and down from month to month. The values on classic toys, however, remain steady and climb gradually, as it is with all items of genuine, not artificial, value.

The real purpose of this book, as with all my books, is to avoid getting a real job by living off royalties and personal appearance fees. No wait. I mean, the real, REAL purpose of this book is to bring back the fun of being a kid by showing you all the cool stuff you had, wish you had, or are discovering for the first time.

WANT TO CONTRIBUTE?

If you have rare toys you'd like to see in future editions of this book (or sequels) contact me at jmars@toyzilla.com and visit my website at www.toyzilla.com or write me at P.O. Box 340, Rancocas, NJ 08073.

Got all that? Good!

It's alive! It's alliiiiive!!!!

While the classic monsters languished in Europe and America in the late 1960s/early 1970s, Mexico was using them to spice up their masked wrestler epics, like *Santo And Blue Demon vs. Dracula and The Wolf Man*. This lobby card is worth $20-25. *Courtesy of Marshall Archives.*

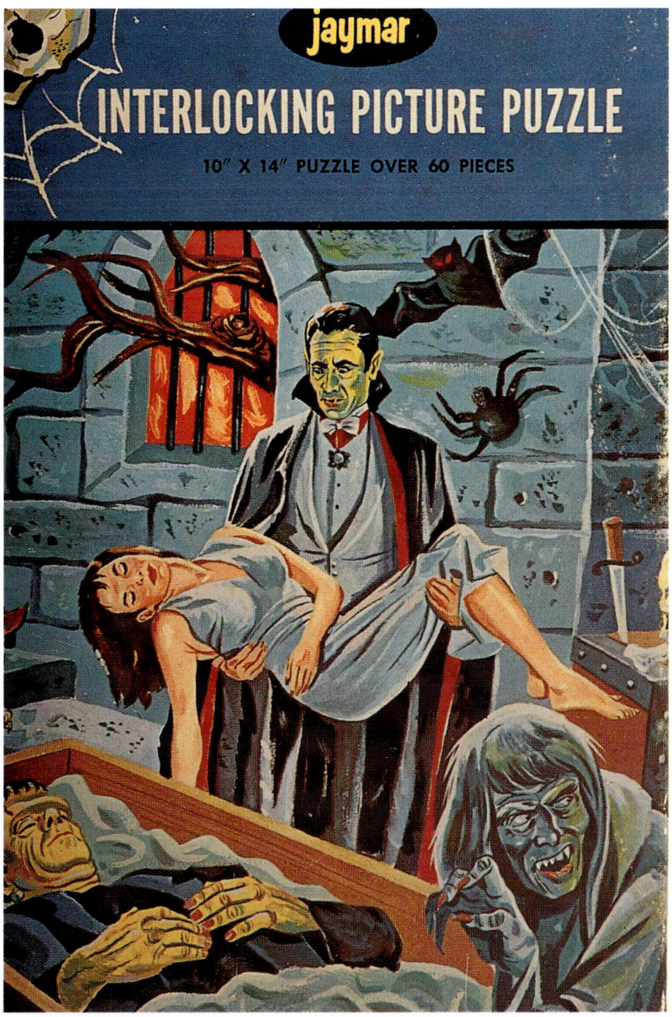

Detail shot of the cover of a 1966 Jaymar Dracula puzzle, $60-70. *Courtesy of Play With This.*

There are many monster mags, but only one monster paper—*The Monster Times*, from the early 1970s. $20-25. *Courtesy of Marshall Archives.*

Detail shot of a Jaymar Wolf Man puzzle, showing guest monster Frankenstein (or, technically, Frankenstein's Monster). $50-60. *Courtesy of Play With This.*

My friend Elisabeth Delliponti (age 5) loaned these cars out to me to photograph for my book. Are YOU gonna tell her no? Neither was I. *Courtesy of Elisabeth Maria Delliponti.*

An Uncle Creepy button from Warren Publications. Unc was the host of *Creepy* magazine, which was filled with illustrated horror stories. $15-20. *Courtesy of Nick Delliponti.*

Cousin Eerie was Uncle Creepy's rival in *Eerie* magazine. $15-20. *Courtesy of Nick Delliponti.*

Another detail from Jaymar's Dracula puzzle shows a typical reader of John Marshall toy books. Way to go, Sister! *Courtesy of Play With This.*

Chapter 1. UNIVERSAL MONSTER TOYS

Let's face it, when it comes to monsters, the ghoul folks at Universal Studios have given us the single best crop of creatures ever to grace a toy shelf.

Of course, Universal didn't invent monster movies. Murnau's German silent epic *Nosferatu* is well-known as the first major vampire flick. And Frankenstein's story had already been well-explored on film, including an illuminating adaptation by Thomas Edison in 1910.

But when Universal turned its attention to horror, it set the standards for all monster movies to come.

It all started, really, with Bela Blasko. In 1931, Universal released a film version of the popular stage play *Dracula*, the story of an aristocratic count who was also a vampire, and his attempts to bring a young woman under his domination. It starred a Hungarian actor who had perfected the role on stage, a man named Bela Blasko. But the world knew him as Bela Lugosi.

In the wake of *Dracula's* success, Universal decided to film a lavish version of Mary Shelley's novel *Frankenstein, Or, The Modern Prometheus*, about a doctor who was able to reanimate a collection of sewn-together body parts. A character actor named William Henry Pratt gladly accepted the role that Bela Lugosi foolishly turned down, and went on to become Boris Karloff, the monarch of horror.

Marx' miniature windup Walking Frankenstein, 1960s. $40-50 loose, $200-250 packaged. *Courtesy of Toyrareum Collectible Toys.*

In the 1940s, there was a second horror boom, which brought forth the popular version of The Mummy as a shambling, bandage covered zombie. It also gave us Larry Talbot, the Wolf Man, expertly played by Creighton Chaney, who had accepted the mantle of Lon Chaney, Junior.

The 1950s saw a wave of new horrors, and chief among them was the *Creature from the Black Lagoon*, who spent three movies battling the humans who dared disturb him in his watery domain.

In the late 1950s and early 1960s, these films were syndicated to television and an entire generation of kids was turned on to the antics of the classic monsters. Slowly, toy makers twigged the idea that the monsters were heroic figures to the kids, and could be merchandised. Marx released a walking, battery-operated Frankenstein early in the decade, with much success.

The Aurora model kit company took a chance on a figural kit of the Frankenstein monster, which resulted in huge sales and an entire line of monster models that continued on successfully for a decade and a half in various incarnations.

Following Aurora's lead, Multiple Products Corporation (MPC) released several different lines of toy soldier-like figures of famous movie monsters, mostly Universal. Some were Pop Top Horrors, figures whose heads came attached to the sides of their bodies on plastic sprues. The heads could be interchanged. The line was not licensed by Universal, but it did include figures who resembled those classic characters. Palmer Plastics had an even more impressive line that incorporated characters like Gorgo and the Cyclops from *The Seventh Voyage of Sinbad.* They also issued some of the figures in "flat" versions, making them smaller and less three-dimensional. (They were more like relief figures than statues.) Most regular Palmers run $20-30 these days, with "flats" in the $10-12 range.

By the mid-1960s, Universal had licensed its monsters' images out for an enormous number of board games and paint-by-number sets from Hasbro and other companies. There were Soaky bubble bath containers by Palmolive and PEZ dispensers. Also, Jaymar had puzzles and other picture-oriented material available.

The mid-1960s saw the Universal monsters losing ground to spy toys and super hero toys, and, in general, in view of the space program and rapidly-increasing modern technology, Universal's monsters were becoming out of date.

Mego's unlicensed yet impressive Frankenstein is seen here in a rare window-front box. $300-400. *Courtesy of Toyrareum Collectible Toys.*

Most Mego 8" Frankenstein figures came in solid boxes. $200-250. The figures came in protective clear bags inside the boxes. Loose $40-50. *Courtesy of Timmy's Toy Dungeon, Inc.*

Ironically, it was in this period that other companies' revivals of these characters were really coming into their own. Since Universal did not own copyrights on the names Frankenstein and Dracula, and since "wolf man" and "mummy" are generic terms, other companies could produce films based on the same or similar characters. England's Hammer Studios trotted out Dracula, Frankenstein, and the Mummy, making Christopher Lee and Peter Cushing household names in the process. Foreign-made films, like *Assignment: Terror* with Michael Rennie, included multiple monsters such as a vampire, a wolfman, a mummy, and the "Franksellan Monster." The Mexicans pitted their masked heroes against an endless horde of vampires, werewolves, and undead menaces. So there was still quite an interest in the classic monsters, even if the Universal marketing machine had run out of steam.

In 1969, Aurora tried to revamp their model kits with Frightening Lightning, a special feature that provided glowing heads, hands, and accessories to its existing models. At first, nobody noticed because the boxes were still the same size and shape. Realizing the error, Aurora quickly switched to fancy square-box packaging and altered box art for their original models, which made the kits more eye-catching on store shelves. The original Frightening Lightning kits in the original boxes are worth half-again as much as the square box glow kits.

Aurora also combined monsters and hot rods models with Frankenstein's Flivver, Mummy's Chariot, Dracula's Dragster and Wolfman's Wagon.

Frankenstein-ish Monster from MPC's 3" plastic figures (1960s). $20-25. *Courtesy of Timmy's Toy Dungeon, Inc.*

My personal favorite Universal Monsters toy was Aurora's line of Monster Scenes kits, an entire world of mad scientist laboratories and torture chambers in which you create your own monster movie scenes. Figures included Frankenstein, Vampirella, a mad scientist named Dr. Deadly, and a voluptuous female Victim who was released in Canada as Dr. Deadly's Daughter. Parental objections to the kits' rather torturous content put an early end to the line in the U.S., but it continued in Canada with Dracula, Dr. Jeckyll and Mr. Hyde, and a Giant Insect which was a cross between a wasp and a scorpion.

But the highlight of the series was its four diorama kits. The Pain Parlor featured a lab table and skeleton; Gruesome Goodies was a complete lab, with electrical generator and test tubes. The Hanging Cage was a deadly trap for the Victim, complete with a brazier of hot coals and torture implements. The Pendulum was a deadly blade that swung back and forth across its victim, which earned it a "Fickle Finger of Fate" award on Laugh-In. These kits are extremely rare, and boxed examples range in the $100-150 area, except for Vampirella ($200-250) and Frankenstein ($300-350).

The Universal Monsters got a big boost in the 1970s when Mego produced a Mad Monster series of action figures. Even though the line was unlicensed, so that Mego did not use the actual Karloff, Lugosi, and Chaney characters, it proved that vampires and werewolves could still sell to kids as action figures.

Not long after, Azrak-Hamway International (A.H.I.) and Lincoln both produced figure lines licensed by Universal. Lincoln made six poseable 8-inch characters of Frankenstein, Dracula, the Mummy, the Wolf Man, the Phantom of the Opera, and the Hunchback. (These were the first proper action figures of the Phantom and the Hunchback.) These six figures are almost impossible to find, and generally run $100-150 loose and $250-300 carded.

AHI (now Remco) produced licensed figures Frankenstein, the Wolf Man, the Mummy and Creature From the Black Lagoon in the 8" size. The first version of the Creature was fully-poseable and plastic, looking like a green version of Johnny Sokko's robot. A second version, sometimes called the "female" creature by idiots, was slimmer, and featured bendy arms and legs (wires with rubber coating). Later they dropped the Creature and added Dracula. Each character went through several head design changes as well as packaging changes.

In 1975, Aurora completely relaunched its figure kits with the all-new Monsters of the Movies line. The Universal monsters in this line included Frankenstein, the Wolf Man, the Creature, and also figures of Dracula, Dr. Jeckyll, and Mr. Hyde, which had originally been planned as additions to the American Monster Scenes line. (The Japanese giants Ghidrah and Rodan were also included.) Astonishingly, the excellent Monsters of the Movies series was a mediocre seller and the line was canceled before kits of Gort (*The Day The Earth Stood Still*), the Metaluna Mutant (*This Island Earth*) and The Fly could be added. These super rare kits easily run $250-300 boxed, with the one common kit, Dr. Jeckyll, running about half of that.

With all the action figure and model kit stuff going on, you'd think that Universal would have taken notice and merchandised their characters more heavily in the 1970s. But Universal only really got into the swing of things in 1979/1980, assigning Remco the task of releasing nine-inch

Here's Aurora's glow-in-the-dark Frankenstein. The original 1960s version runs $40-50 built up, and $200-250 boxed. This version, from the early 1970s, runs about half of that. *Courtesy of Toyrareum Collectible Toys.*

tall action figures with accordion-like crusher grip. They also released pocket-sized figures and the extremely rare "Monsters At Home" line of finger puppets who came in little "homes" (a coffin for Dracula, a sarcophagus for The Mummy, etc.)

Unlike many other character collectible lines, the Universal monsters have seen most of their best merchandise produced not a long time ago, but rather, in the last ten or fifteen years. Advances in manufacturing have allowed for better likenesses and cooler KINDS of merchandise to be produced in the images of the classic monsters.

In the year 1991, we saw the sixtieth anniversary of the release of *Dracula* and *Frankenstein*, and it was from this point on that Universal has made an enormous push to continually keep its famous monsters at the forefront of the public's attention. Every year, especially around Halloween, exciting new products come out, and manufacturers constantly find new ways to "cool-ify" the classics.

There simply is no escaping the curse of Universal's Monsters. You are doomed to love the characters, and while other monsters may come and go as fads dictate, Dracula, Frankie, Wolfie and the Creech will continually rise up to terrorize the toy shelves for the rest of eternity.

Aurora also experimented with hot rods for monsters. Here's Frankenstein's Flivver. Built Up $100-150. Boxed $300-400. *Courtesy of Toyrareum Collectible Toys.*

The best-loved of all movie monsters, Frankie is a perennial Halloween favorite. Here's a 1970s costume that's "Night-Owl Bright" for easy visibility. MIP $30-40. *Courtesy of Timmy's Toy Dungeon, Inc.*

The costume looks cool laid out— ON THE SLAB! NYAHAHAHAHA!!! Loose $20-25. *Courtesy of Timmy's Toy Dungeon, Inc.*

Azrak-Hamway International (later Remco) made a series of 8" licensed monster figures in the mid-1970s. This Frankie, from Paul Levitt's collection, once graced the cover of *Collecting Toys* magazine. Loose $50-60. MIP $250-300.

Funstuff made two super-rare inflatable figures. Dracula was one, and here's Frankenstein, with his lab table. Loose $50-60. MIP $125-150. *Courtesy of Kollector's Choice.*

A close-up of the gruesome glowing head. *Courtesy of Kollector's Choice.*

Vics, in 1979, made rubber 6" monsters, like Frankie here. Loose $15-18. Carded $30-40. *Courtesy of Toyrareum Collectible Toys.*

Here's Remco's 1979 Frankenstein boxed. $70-80. *Courtesy of Toyrareum Collectible Toys.*

And here he is unboxed, $30-40. *Courtesy of Paul Levitt.*

The Universals, and Frankie especially, have always lent themselves well to goofy interpretations for games and such. $12-15. *Courtesy of Play With This.*

Detail of the faces. *Courtesy of Play With This.*

This creepy walking Frank is fairly recent, a 1990s issue from Robot House. $100-125. *Courtesy of Toyrareum Collectible Toys.*

And here's his box. *Courtesy of Toyrareum Collectible Toys.*

Left:
Universal licensing exploded in the 1990s. This Frankie watch is a good example of some of the lower-priced merchandise. $10-12. *Courtesy of Toyrareum Collectible Toys.*

Many playthings feature frighteningly-accurate likenesses, like this 1980s rubber head. $15-18. *Courtesy of Kollector's Choice.*

Imperial did a nice job in the mid-1980s with four vinyl monster figures that stood roughly 8" high. Frankie's $10-12 loose, $15-18 carded. *Courtesy of Toyrareum Collectible Toys.*

He's escaped! *Courtesy of Paul Levitt.*

Frankie's even cuddly! This "stuffy" is a 1990s invention, $5-6. *Courtesy of Play With This.*

For the 1991 anniversaries of the Universal Frankenstein and Dracula movies, Just Toys released a series of bendy beasties. Frankenstein's $5-6 loose and $12-15 carded. *Courtesy of Play With This.*

Universal's uglies have graced many a puzzle, from the 1960s through this mid-1990s example, an especially arresting Frankie. $10-12. *Courtesy of Timmy's Toy Dungeon, Inc.*

The monsters got a 1990s action figure treatment with Monster Force. Frank was a late release and hard to find. Loose $5-6. MIP $15-19. *Courtesy of Play With This.*

The 1990s brought great new gimmicks to Universal monster merchandising. This fast-food Frankie has a lab table with a light that shines through his translucent head. Loose $2-3. MIP $5-6. *Courtesy of Nick Delliponti.*

My personal favorite 1990s Frankie thing is this vibrating electric chair. Loose $10-12. MIP $20-25. *Courtesy of Nick Delliponti.*

Another "funny" Frank is this Just Toys bendy from the 1990s. $5-6 as shown. *Courtesy of Paul Levitt.*

Scarier (and less poseable) is this 1990s PVC figurette. $5-6. *Courtesy of Toyrareum Collectible Toys.*

Everyone knows that the cartoon *The Real Ghostbusters* was better than the movies. They did a line of pseudo-Universal monsters, including this Frankenstein. $5-6 loose, $15-18 carded. *Courtesy of Paul Levitt.*

Stepping back a few years we have this View Master. $12-15. *Courtesy of Paul Levitt.*

And back to the 1960s, when this Frankie head once graced a hollow vinyl Troll body. Don't despair—you can pop the head onto a G. I. Joe! As shown $10-12. *Courtesy of Paul Levitt.*

In the 1990s, everything old was new again. Playing Mantis reissued Frank's Flivver and many other models under the name Polar Lights. They also used almost exact copies of the original boxes. $15-20. *Courtesy of Nick Delliponti.*

Frank and Drac team up on this early 1980s movie viewer. Loose $6-8 complete. MIP $15-18. *Courtesy of Play With This.*

Here's an original 1960s Aurora Dracula kit. Built Up $80-90. MIP $400-500. The 1970s version is worth about half that. *Courtesy of Toyrareum Collectible Toys.*

Palmer made various plastic figures of monsters, in different scales, in the 1960s. Here's their "flat" version Dracula. $5-6. *Courtesy of Timmy's Toy Dungeon, Inc.*

Detail of the bat-faced dog. Brrrrr. *Courtesy of Play With This.*

Jaymar's 1960s puzzles are notorious for their gruesome content and multiple monsters. $60-70. *Courtesy of Play With This.*

AHI's 8" Dracula from the mid-1970s shrugs because not only is his cape missing, but AHI replaced Creature from the Black Lagoon with him when they lost their Universal license. (Dracula's name isn't trademarked but the Creature's is.) *Courtesy of Toyrareum Collectible Toys.*

A Dracula kit of an entirely different stake was Japanese produced in the 1980s. $20-25. *Courtesy of Paul Levitt.*

Left:
Count Chockula has become as well-known as his Transylvanian counterpart. Here's a collectible vinyl figure from the 1970s. $15-18. *Courtesy of Play With This.*

Right:
As I said, the 1990s have been very good to these monsters. The Motionette series brought large, doll-like characters to life via motion and sound. Drac is $20-25 loose, $40-50 boxed. *Courtesy of Play With This.*

Remco's 1980 Dracula figure had glowing head and hands and grabbing action— plus the best cape of any vintage Drac figure. Loose $15-20. MIP $50-60. *Courtesy of Play With This.*

This wax figure of Drac will melt if you put a flame to his wick— let's see Peter Cushing do THAT to Christopher Lee. 1990s. $8-10. *Courtesy of Play With This.*

Left:
Imperial's 1980s Dracula was the best in their line. Loose $10-12. MIP $15-18. *Courtesy of Paul Levitt.*

Right:
Here he is in his colorful package. *Courtesy of Toyrareum Collectible Toys.*

Here's the bendy Drac from Just Toys that goes with the anniversary Frankie. Loose $5-6, MIP $15-18. *Courtesy of Play With This.*

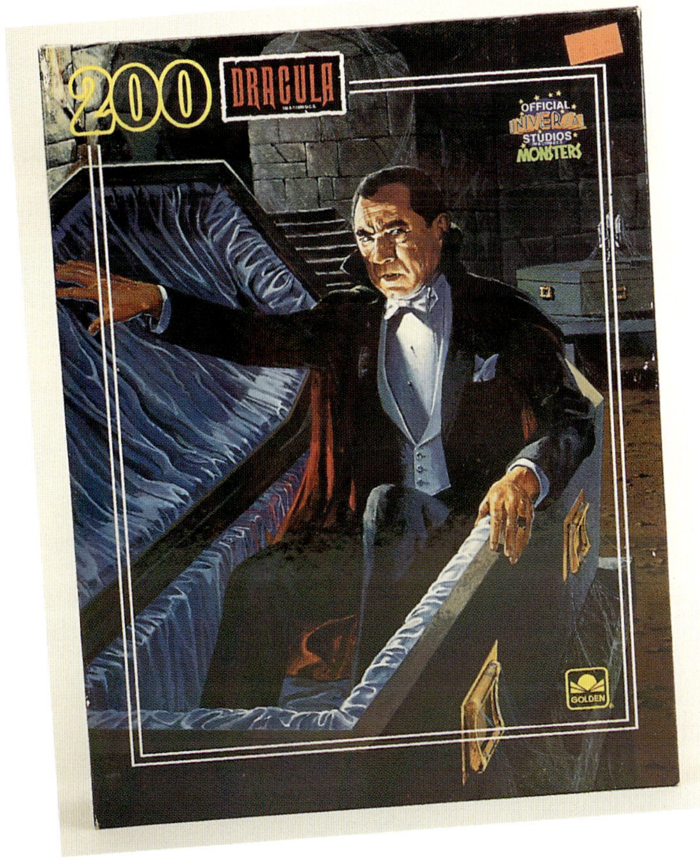

Another great 1990s puzzle, with a great Lugosi pose. $12-15. *Courtesy of Play With This.*

In 1998, we saw one of the best Bela Lugosi figures hit the market. $6-8 loose, carded $15-20. *Courtesy of Aaron Kessler.*

Dracula joins the 1990s watch parade. $10-12. *Courtesy of Toyrareum Collectible Toys.*

Dracula was the leader of the villains who opposed the Monster Force. $5-6 loose, $12-15 carded. *Courtesy of Aaron Kessler.*

Many glasses are expensive, but monster glasses are worth it. This 1960s Wolfie has art all around ...

... including a full moon above a creepy castle. $70-80. *Courtesy of Play With This.*

One of Remco's best figures was its 9" Lon Chaney Wolfman from 1979. The likeness was excellent. Loose $30-40. Boxed $120-150. *Courtesy of Play With This.*

This rubber figure from the 1970s had lots of sculpted detail. $20-30. *Courtesy of Play With This.*

For reasons that anthropologists can't understand, trolls were a big fad in the 1960s. Here are Wolfman and King Kong with the Troll treatment. $10-15 each. *Courtesy of Play With This.*

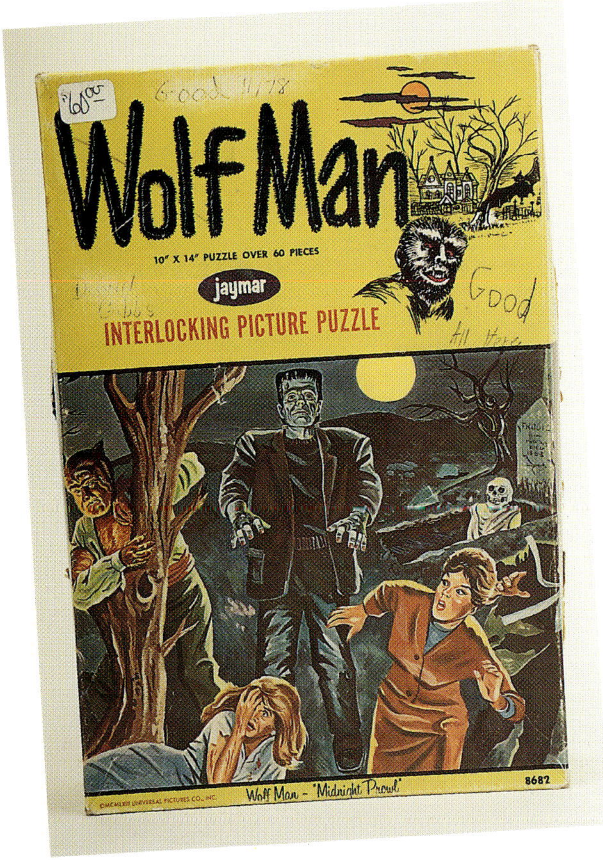

Left:
Another great Jaymar puzzle sees Frankenstein crowding our lupine lovely right out of his own illustration!

Right:
Aah, there he is! $60-70. *Courtesy of Play With This.*

Here's Mego's Wolfman in the rare window box. $300-400. *Courtesy of Toyrareum Collectible Toys.*

The box back shows the illo that also appears on both sides of the "solid" version of the box, which rates $200-250. *Courtesy of Toyrareum Collectible Toys.*

Here's a loose lobo! $60-75. *Courtesy of Paul Levitt.*

That ubiquitous 1970s object, the Book N Record set. Here is Marvel's Werewolf By Night reworked as an audio drama, with a guest appearance by Dracula! $15-20. *Courtesy of Timmy's Toy Dungeon, Inc.*

The 1970s had its share of monster puzzles, although they were understated by Jaymar 1960s standards. $15-20. *Courtesy of Timmy's Toy Dungeon, Inc.*

Here's a bendable Wolfman, standing about six inches, another 1970s offering from AHI. Loose $30-40. MIP $70-80. *Courtesy of Play With This.*

An interesting take (well, a take, anyway) on the werewolf theme was the 1970s cartoon *Fangface*. His board game is $20-25. *Courtesy of Play With This.*

The group of dolls based on Michael Jackson's Thriller (Jackson was a popular 1980s pop singer.) was one strange toy line. Here's the werewolf. Loose $10-12. MIP $18-20. *Courtesy of Play With This.*

In the '90s, monsters were all over the place. This Wolfman shopping bag will set you back a hairy $5-6. *Courtesy of Play With This.*

We previously saw the Dracula Motionette, but this Wolfman is actually a rare GIANT version.

Here he is out of his box. Hairy and scary! $100-125. *Courtesy of Play With This.*

Here's the regular size version of the werewolf in his distinctive box. $50-60. *Courtesy of Paul Levitt.*

The Monster Force Wolfman. Loose $3-4. MIP $12-15. *Courtesy of Play With This.*

Aurora's glow Wolfman kit from the 1970s had box art that resembled the model. $150-200. (The original, which is worth twice as much, had art similar to that of the Wolf Man behind a tree on the Jaymar Wolf Man puzzle.) *Courtesy of Toyrareum Collectible Toys.*

But don't take my word for it, Sparky, see for yourself! Built Up $40-50. Tree limbs and rat tails! *Courtesy of Toyrareum Collectible Toys.*

This View Master retelling of the Wolfman's story is too nicey-nice but the figures and layouts are cool. (Trust me.) $12-15. *Courtesy of Timmy's Toy Dungeon, Inc.*

The Wolfman figure is often the most sought-after in any group of Universal Monsters figures (ones that don't have a Creature, anyway). So it is with Imperial's 1980s Wolfie, which we not only couldn't find carded but we had to settle for this slightly dog-eared specimen. Loose $12-15. Carded $20-25. *Courtesy of Toyrareum Collectible Toys.*

Another MPC figurine from the 1960s is this bat-eared werewolf. Don't use silver bullets, send Mike Tyson after him. $12-15. *Courtesy of Timmy's Toy Dungeon, Inc.*

Or, if licensed Lon likenesses are more in your line of lycanthropy, leer longingly at this Marx statuette from the 1960s, about 5" tall. $20-25. *Courtesy of Toyrareum Collectible Toys.*

The same holds true for this Just Toys bendy. Loose $10-12. Carded $20-25. *Courtesy of Paul Levitt.*

The Japanese love wolf men too, as evidenced by this "egg" character. $6-8 loose, $15-20 boxed. *Courtesy of Paul Levitt.*

Another Polar Lights reissue, this time of Wolfman's Wagon. $15-20. *Courtesy of Nick Delliponti.*

The box for Robot House's 1990s Wolfman is pretty dull... *Courtesy of Toyrareum Collectible Toys.*

... but the robot himself is a lupine lovely in printed steel. $100-125. *Courtesy of Toyrareum Collectible Toys.*

The Aurora Mummy Model, 1960s issue. Built Up, $40-50. MIP $200-250. *Courtesy of Timmy's Toy Dungeon, Inc.*

Mego's leotard-clad mummy was not Universal-inspired, so it resembles more of a Mexican or Italian movie mummy. But Universal collectors love Mego's series anyway. Loose $25-35. MIP $100-125. *Courtesy of Play With This.*

A pair of Palmer Plastics "flat" Mummies. Each $8-10. *Courtesy of Timmy's Toy Dungeon, Inc.*

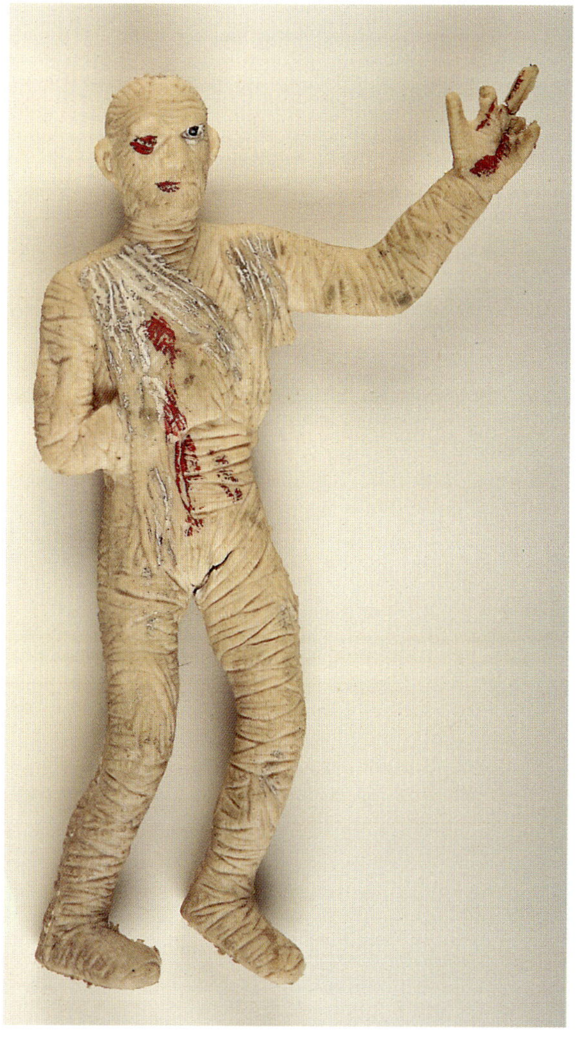

This AHI 1970s rubber Mummy is the best-sculpted Mummster I've ever seen. Loose $20-25. MIP $75-85. *Courtesy of Play With This.*

And this Vic's Mummy from 1979 is the second best rubber Mummy I've ever seen. Loose $15-18. MIP $20-30. *Courtesy of Toyrareum Collectible Toys.*

The Mummy's Chariot is not as popular as other Aurora Hot Rods, but Polar Lights reissued it in the 1990s, not wanting to leave it out. $15-20. *Courtesy of Nick Delliponti.*

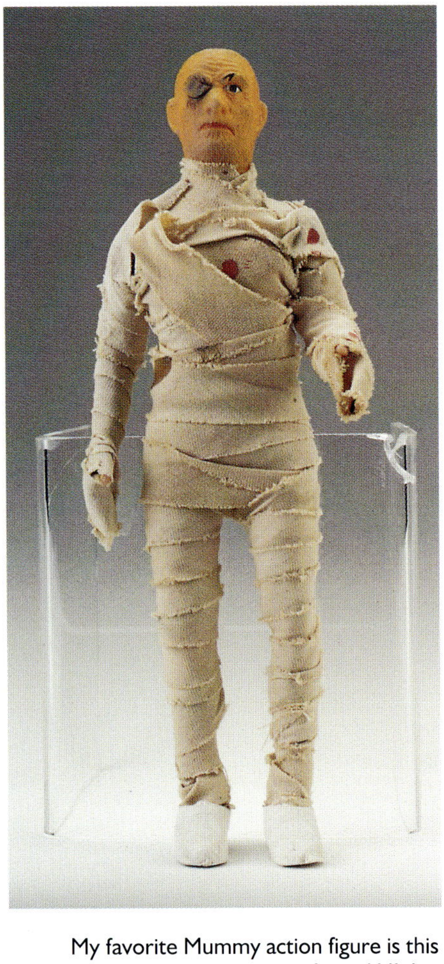

My favorite Mummy action figure is this 1970s Karloffian accident victim from AHI. Loose $40-50. Carded $175-200. *Courtesy of Toyrareum Collectible Toys.*

Another relic from the '70s (1970s) is this Mummy Machine from AMT, reissued in the 1990s by AMT, following Polar Lights' lead. $15-20. *Courtesy of Nick Delliponti.*

This Jim Henson-esque Mummy rates $5-6 as shown. *Courtesy of Paul Levitt.*

This roly-poly Mummy reminds one of Lon Chaney's run as The Bandaged One. $4-5 as shown. *Courtesy of Paul Levitt.*

Remco's 1979 Mummy wasn't great, but like most figures in the line, the face bore an excellent likeness to the actor who played the character (in this case, Boris Karloff). Boxed $70-80. *Courtesy of Play With This.*

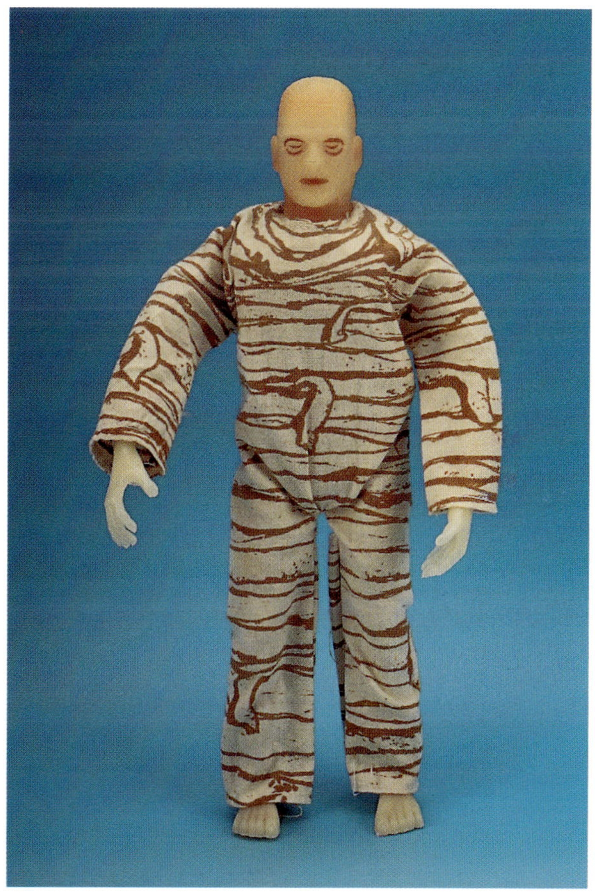

As you can see, great face, but what's up with those mummy jammies? Loose $30-40. *Courtesy of Play With This.*

Why not a Mummy watch? Of any monster who'd want to know what time it was ... $15-20. *Courtesy of Toyrareum Collectible Toys.*

This brownish blob is Just Toys' bendy Mummy from the 1990s. Loose $2-3. MIP $8-10. *Courtesy of Play With This.*

Imperial's Mummy was the weak link in their 1980s figure chain. Loose $6-8. Carded $10-12. *Courtesy of Toyrareum Collectible Toys.*

A Mummy who screams? This mini-motionette was one of a dozen Halloween leftovers that my buddy Tim Welsh picked up at a drugstore for fifty cents apiece. Loose $5-6. MIP $10-15. (Or fifty cents if you can get 'em.) *Courtesy of Timmy's Toy Dungeon, Inc.*

Robot House's Mummy had better box art than the others ...

... but the robot scores the same as all the other robots, a perfect ten. $100-125. *Courtesy of Toyrareum Collectible Toys.*

This 1990s rubber shrunken head is the best Mummy face I've seen yet. Those eyes are creepy! $5-6. *Courtesy of Toyrareum Collectible Toys.*

Aurora's original Creature kit, a true piece of classic plastic. Built Up $60-70. *Courtesy of Timmy's Toy Dungeon, Inc.*

And here he is boxed. $500-600. *Courtesy of Toyrareum Collectible Toys.*

Here's the glow version, $50-60 built up. *Courtesy of Toyrareum Collectible Toys.*

The original Marx creature statuette, in aqua blue. They came in various colors. $20-25. *Courtesy of Timmy's Toy Dungeon, Inc.*

AHI's second-issue Creature action figure, with bendy arms and legs. Loose $200-250. MIP $500-600. The boxier first version's worth about twice as much. *Courtesy of Toyrareum Collectible Toys.*

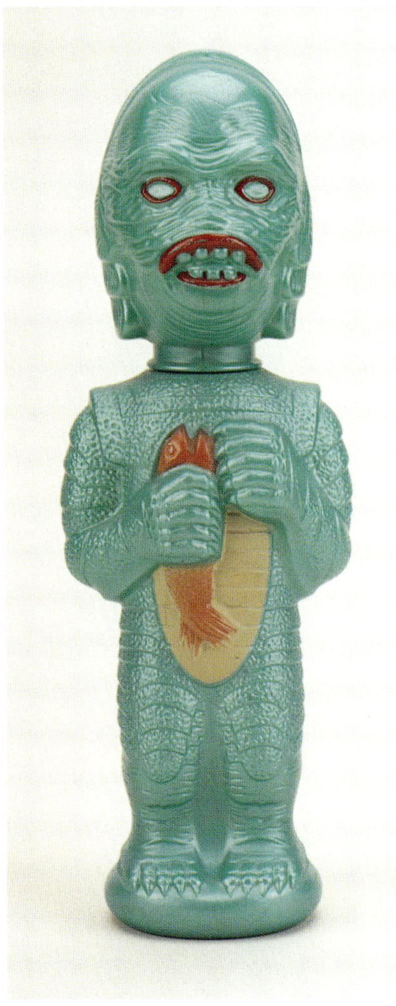

The bathtub is the last place I want to be reminded of an aquatic monster, but I still love this Creature "Soaky" bubble bath container from the 1960s. The fish really makes it. $100-125. *Courtesy of Play With This.*

These Creature windup walkers have been reissued from time to time. The is a 1980s version. $10-12. *Courtesy of Play With This.*

This Creature shrunken head (1990s) is one of the closer likenesses made in a toy image of Creech. $5-6. *Courtesy of Toyrareum Collectible Toys.*

This 1990s key chain has great sculpting. The Creature really lends himself to it, with all those scales. Loose $2-3. Carded $8-10. *Courtesy of Play With This.*

Now THAT's what I call appropriate. This 1990s Creature water ball paper weight fetches $20-25 loose and $30-35 boxed. *Courtesy of Play With This.*

This 1990s Creech costume was picked up on after-Halloween sale for $1.25 the same day that Tim bought the fifty-cent screaming Mummies. $20-25. *Courtesy of Timmy's Toy Dungeon, Inc.*

This Creature shopping bag may or may not be the flip side of the previously shown Wolfman shopping bag. $3-5. *Courtesy of Play With This.*

The Monster Force Creature was their best piece. Loose $3-4. MIP $12-15. *Courtesy of Play With This*

Creech waves hello on his Robot House box lid. *Courtesy of Toyrareum Collectible Toys.*

And look how great he is in the metal! $125-150. *Courtesy of Toyrareum Collectible Toys.*

For a while you could get these Creech puzzles in any dollar store. Not any more. $12-15. *Courtesy of Timmy's Toy Dungeon, Inc.*

This Big Head Creech is a perfect example of how most Universal Monsters merchandise was produced in a high standard as the 1990s drew to a close. Loose $5-6. Carded $12-15. *Courtesy of Marshall Archives.*

The *Monster Squad* was a Saturday-morning 1970s series created by the team behind the 1966 *Batman* show. It pitted Drac, Frank, and Wolfie against assorted villains, including Jonathan Harris as an evil wizard. (Or was that *Ghost Busters?*) $20-25. *Courtesy of Play With This.*

Here's the game board. *Courtesy of Play With This.*

And the Creature! "HISSS!!!"

One overlooked 1990s item is the figural key chain series. Nick Delliponti picked these up at a dollar store. Here's Wolfman! "AARRROOOOO!!!"

And Dr. Acula! "I vant to bite your finger!"

And Frankenstein's Monster! "Friend, gooood!"

And the Bride of Frankenstein's monster! "Jennifer Beals I'm not!"

And The Mummy! ".......!!!!" Each is $2-3 loose, $8-10 carded. *Courtesy of Nick Delliponti.*

Penn-Plax reissued the old Marx Monsters in the early 1990s in glow in the dark plastic. Each rates $4-5 loose, $10-12 carded. *Courtesy of Paul Levitt.c*

Want to know why?

There was a rumor that they were NOT made of non-toxic plastic and had to be pulled; but, it hasn't really affected their value.

Largely due to the presence of this set of tan colored (and paintable) Aurora reissues, manufactured at the same time. This set was produced in large quantities and collectibles dealers still sell them for around $20 a set (of six). *Courtesy of Paul Levitt.*

This 1979 lunch box stands out as one of the all-time great Universal Monsters items. Not only is the art great, but EVERYBODY'S HERE! Here's Ygor performing the nuptials ...

... the Mummy creeps on a side panel ...

... the Phantom and the under-used Metaluna Mutant skulk up the other side ...

... Leo G. Carroll from Tarantula and a Mole Person guard the handle ...

... Creech protects the bottom ...

... *and* Dracula and Wolfman keep watch on the other side! $20-25. *Courtesy of Play With This.*

This Fast Food Dracula from the 1990s popped up out of his coffin—like Nosferatu. Loose $2-3. MIP $5-6. *Courtesy of Nick Delliponti.*

Aurora's 1960s Phantom of the Opera kit is $50-60 built up and $200-250 boxed ...

Below:
... while its Glow reissue is $40-50 built up and $125-150 boxed. *Courtesy of Toyrareum Collectible Toys.*

Here's Wolfman and Creature, from the fast food series. Each Loose $2-3. MIP $5-6. *Courtesy of Nick Delliponti.*

The whole set of Shrunken heads, produced in the 1990s. $30-40. *Courtesy of Toyrareum Collectible Toys.*

Aurora's Bride of Frankenstein was never reissued in the 1970s. Built Up $300-400. Boxed $800-900. *Courtesy of Toyrareum Collectible Toys.*

A recent Monster edible is this box of cookies, which I "emptied out" before shooting. Any excuse to eat! $3-4. *Courtesy of Marshall Raided Pantry.*

Carded Remco Mini-Monsters 1980 Glow Frankenstein. Loose $10-12. Carded $30-40. *Courtesy of Toyrareum Collectible Toys.*

Carded Remco Mini-Monsters Wolfman, 1980. Loose $20-25. Carded $50-60. *Courtesy of Toyrareum Collectible Toys.*

Carded Remco Mini-Monsters Glow Dracula, 1980. Loose $12-15. Carded $25-30. *Courtesy of Toyrareum Collectible Toys.*

Carded Remco Mini-Monsters Mummy, 1980. Loose $10-15. Carded $30-40. *Courtesy of Toyrareum Collectible Toys.*

Carded Creature mini-monster, 1980. Loose $15-20. Carded $40-50. *Courtesy of Toyrareum Collectible Toys.*

Carded glow in the dark mini-Creature, 1980. Loose $15-20. Carded $40-450. *Courtesy of Toyrareum Collectible Toys.*

Carded Glow in the Dark mini Phantom, 1980. Loose $12-15. Carded $30-40. *Courtesy of Play With This.*

And a house to put them in! The Remco Mini-Monster Play Case. 1980. $30-40. *Courtesy of Paul Levitt.*

Chapter 2. CLASSIC MONSTERS OF MOVIES AND TV

King Kong was the first great monster movie produced by a movie studio other than Universal. That big ape starred in one of the most highly-praised movies ever made, one which routinely lands on All-Time Top Ten lists. And why not? It has it all—action, drama, and romance—and an interspecies romance at that.

Kids' merchandising for *King Kong* started in the 1960s with Aurora's jaw-dropping model and Palmer's cool figurine. KK continued to visit toyland from time to time after that, but in 1976 the Dino DeLaurentis remake caused a Kong-sized wave of merchandise. Today, the ol' gorilla is still a beloved, much respected character who, from time to time, gets a toy made in his likeness.

Aurora's King Kong kit, original 1960s issue. Built Up $100-125. Boxed $450-500. *Courtesy of Timmy's Toy Dungeon, Inc.*

Ray Harryhausen, the effects master who gave us those great Sinbad movies, has only seen his creations turn up occasionally as toys. The Palmer Plastics 1960s Cyclops ($20-25) and the 1970s Sinbad board game ($70-80), are rare exceptions. But in 1981, there was a merchandising push for Harryhausen's final epic, *Clash of The Titans*, and we have some of that stuff here.

While the non-Universal classic monster movies had sparse merchandising, TV's monsters fared much better. It was inevitable that monsters would become a staple of television programming. It was equally inevitable that the monsters of TV would turn up on merchandise aimed at kids.

In 1964, TV producer Irwin Allen was cranking out monster oriented adventure shows like *Lost In Space*, so TV icons like the L.I.S. Cyclops turned up on merchandising.

Star Trek was no stranger to monsters, although they only turned up on rare occasions. *Dr. Who* employed them more often, although *Dr. Who* toys have mostly been produced overseas and are hard to find.

The seventies gave America *The Monster Squad*, in the persons of Frankenstein, Dracula, and the Wolfman, who battled baddies for a season of Saturday mornings in the early 1970s.

Space: 1999 was monster-lite in its first season; but, they more than made up for it in the monster-filled second season in an attempt to attract more kids to the show.

Then we have that cultural phenomenon known as *Planet of the Apes*, which has spawned five feature films, a one-season live-action TV series, and a one-season animated TV series.

And there we have, I think, quite a miscellany of monsters!

The 1970s "glow" version of the kit. Kong came with various alternate glow body parts, but the modeler chose to use just the glowing Fay Wray. Built Up $50-60. Boxed $200-300. *Courtesy of Toyrareum Collectible Toys.*

Rubbery 1970s King Kong, $15-20. *Courtesy of Timmy's Toy Dungeon, Inc.*

Roly-sparky Kong from Japan, 1980s. $5-6. *Courtesy of Paul Levitt.*

Palmer's King Kong 3" figure from the 1960s. $25-30. *Courtesy of Timmy's Toy Dungeon, Inc.*

A 1960s King Kong troll, with no tuft of hair so you can see his cool head. $15-20. *Courtesy of Play With This.*

1970s King Kong bank, $30-40. *Courtesy of Play With This.*

The 1976 *King Kong* film inspired its fair share of merchandise. Here's the board game. $20-25. *Courtesy of Play With This.*

King Kong gum machine ring, 1960s. $30-40. *Courtesy of Timmy's Toy Dungeon, Inc.*

The object of the game was to move Kong up the twin towers. *Courtesy of Play With This.*

When Dino De Laurentis explained his idea for a sequel, with Kong revived like Frankenstein, people thought he was kidding. But *King Kong Lives* went on to become a major flop of the 1980s. Belt Buckle, $15-20. *Courtesy of Timmy's Toy Dungeon, Inc.*

Heroine Jessica Lange, went on to win the Best Actress Oscar. (Not for *King Kong*, though.) See her emote on these View Masters, $20-25. *Courtesy of Timmy's Toy Dungeon, Inc.*

Right:
This 1980s salt and pepper shaker set is more of a novelty than a toy. Write me and complain. $20-25. *Courtesy of Play With This.*

This puzzle gives you hundreds of pieces of Kong, which is just what the NYC Public Works Department had to carry away in garbage bags. $15-20. *Courtesy of Timmy's Toy Dungeon, Inc.*

This 1970s stuffed Kong is the larger of two versions, being about 15" tall. He's $30-40. His little brother, about 12" tall, is $20-30. *Courtesy of Toyrareum Collectible Toys.*

The second in our series of winding sparky walkers from the 1980s, Kong fetches $10-12. *Courtesy of Play With This.*

This skateboarding King Kong is recent and probably unlicensed. It's $2-3 loose and $5-6 MIP. *Courtesy of Play With This.*

This Imperial hard rubber King Kong is of recent vintage but an excellent likeness. Loose $6-8. Tagged $12-15. *Courtesy of Play With This.*

But, if you look closely, it's an amazing likeness of the Toho version of King Kong from *King Kong vs. Godzilla*.

He may not look like it, but this Cyclops from Combex' Famous Monsters of Legend line (1970s) is based (loosely) on the one in *The Seventh Voyage of Sinbad*. Loose $20-25. MIP $150-175. MIP (Star Raiders packaging 1978) $80-90. *Courtesy of Play With This.*

The game board shows several of the monsters. *Courtesy of Play With This.*

Most Ray Harryhausen monsters were not merchandised much when they were "new." One exception was the gang from *Clash of the Titans* (1981). The board game is worth $25-30. *Courtesy of Play With This.*

This detail shows a Medusa card, which is a rare Medusa-related image. (There were no toys of her.) *Courtesy of Play With This.*

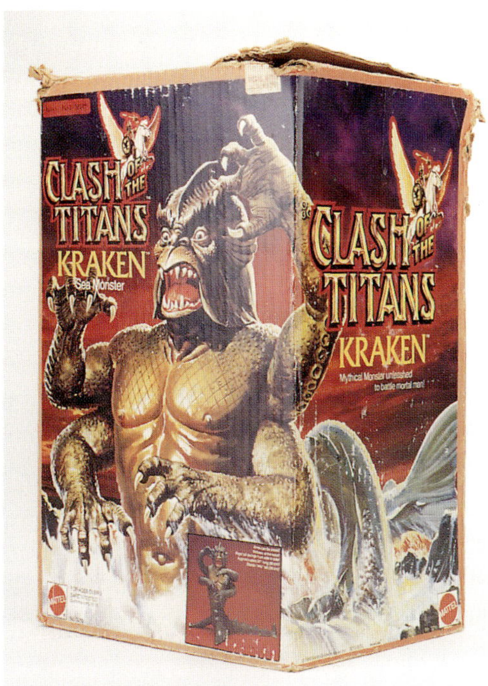

Mattel's *Clash of The Titans* action figure line, though not especially well-done, is popular with monster collectors because it's the only licensed action figure series based on a Harryhausen film. Boxed Kraken $150-200. *Courtesy of Toyrareum Collectible Toys.*

Here you can see he's rather "plasticy." His feet-fins, once snapped on, can't be removed without breaking them, which makes it impossible to get Kracky back in his box. Loose $80-90. *Courtesy of Toyrareum Collectible Toys.*

This Saucer Man (from *Invasion Of The Saucer Men*) was part of a 1990s fast food meal premium. $5-6. *Courtesy of Nick Delliponti.*

A friend of the Combex Cyclops is this Combex Morlock from *The Time Machine*—or he would have been, if the licensing had gone through. Loose $30-40. Carded (Famous Monsters of Legend) $150-200. Carded (Star Raiders) $70-80. *Courtesy of Play With This.*

For the most part, I consider 1980s-1990s vinyl kits to be objects duh art, intended for modelers and collectors, not kids' toys. But Billiken did such a great job on this Saucer Man I knew you'd want to see it. $80-90. *Courtesy of Paul Levitt.*

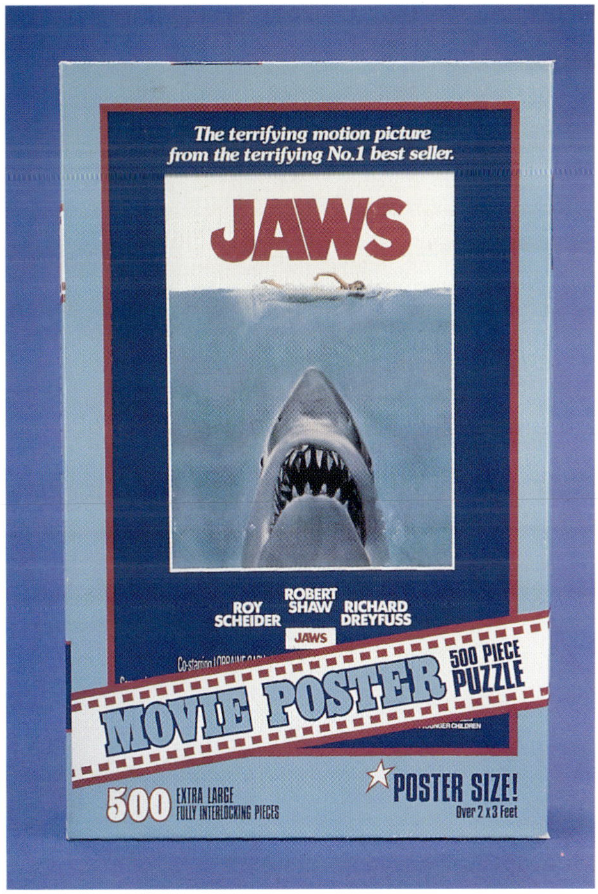

Left:
Jaws inspired more toys than I'd imagined. I do remember this Jaws game.

Right:
The movie poster made for a great puzzle. $12-15. *Courtesy of Timmy's Toy Dungeon, Inc.*

Below:
The object of the game was to carefully snatch garbage from his mouth, which could snap shut at any time! $25-30. *Courtesy of Kollector's Choice.*

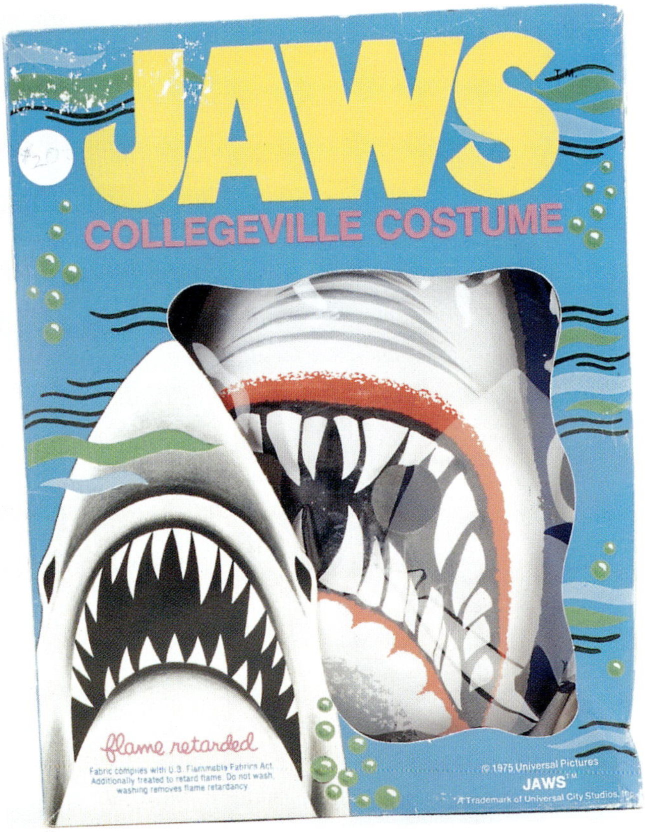

Many of today's executives wore this costume for Halloween as kids in 1975. Loose $20-25. MIP $40-50. *Courtesy of Toyrareum Collectible Toys.*

The Jaws costume in all its carcharodonian glory. *Courtesy of Toyrareum Collectible Toys.*

Star Wars gave us lots of great aliens and villains, but only one true monster— the Rancor! Here, two Rancors debate the virtues of Liebnitz over Vichtenstein. Loose $25-30. Boxed $80-90. *Courtesy of Nick Delliponti.*

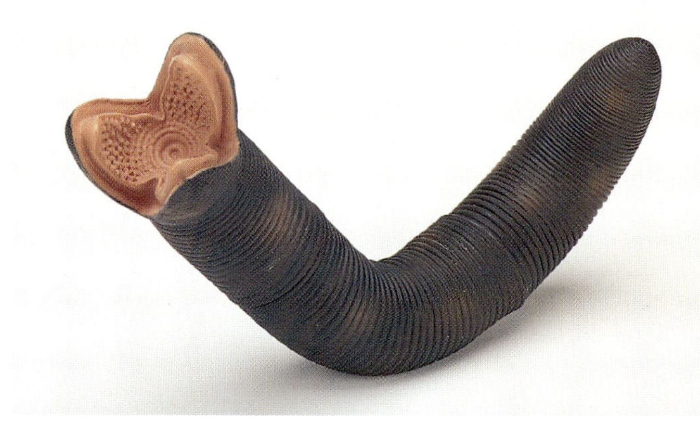

Okay, go ahead, make your little jokes about this object. Done now? Good. It's really a *Dune* Sandworm, 1980s. Loose $12-15. MIP $40-50. *Courtesy of Play With This.*

LuluBelle, the famous two-headed seaweed beast, terrorized both *Lost In Space* and *Voyage* on numerous occasions. Here she is on the View Master pack. $30-40. *Courtesy of Play With This.*

Kids of the 1960s who yearned for more Irwin Allen monster toys had to grow up, start toy companies, and make their own. That's why we have this 1998 Trendmasters version of a 1965 *Lost In Space* Cyclops. Loose $12-15. MIP $30-35. *Courtesy of Marshall Archives.*

She was also featured in the story booklet's art. *Courtesy of Play With This.*

Here's the *Lost In Space* Cyclops doing his thing in an original Aurora 1960s kit. Built Up $200-300. MIP $700-800. Version with Chariot, add 50% to values. *Courtesy of Timmy's Toy Dungeon, Inc.*

Two views of the Aurora *Land of the Giants* snake scene kit ...

Which one of you little figures is Deanna Lund, anyway? Built Up $200-250. MIP $400-500. *Courtesy of Timmy's Toy Dungeon, Inc.*

Star Trek wasn't a big monster show, but we ran across this Spock vs. Snake scene from the 1970s and thought you'd like to see it.

Here is a better view of the three-headed snake. Built Up $30-40. Boxed $100-125. *Courtesy of Toyrareum Collectible Toys.*

This Gorn is another classic *Star Trek* monster we can't get enough of. This PVC figure is from the early 1990s. $5-6. *Courtesy of Paul Levitt.* The only pre-1990s Gorn item is the Mego 8" doll, but all he is is a brown Lizard head on an Apes body wearing Klingon clothes. So there!

Likewise for the Mugato ($5-6), except HIS Mego figure was made of mostly-new parts—and came dressed in a darling green suit ... for no particular reason. *Courtesy of Paul Levitt.*

... with a working ghost! Boxed $500-600. *Courtesy of Toyrareum Collectible Toys.*

It must be a museum, 'cause its the Addams Family House by Aurora. Built Up $300-400 ...

Remco's Morticia big-head statue from the 1960s. $40-50 as shown. C'est belle, no? John! That's French! (Followed by me kissing myself on the arm.) *Courtesy of Toyrareum Collectible Toys.*

Here in John Marshall Land, we believe firmly that "Something Is Better Than Nothing." In that gran espiritu, we bring you the head of a Morticia Addams hand puppet (1960s). Complete puppet $70-80. MIP $150-200. *Courtesy of Toyrareum Collectible Toys.*

The Thing Bank, boxed. It's a black box and Thing pops out to take your money and add it to the Addams fortune. $100-125. *Courtesy of Toyrareum Collectible Toys.*

The side panel shows the whole Addams clan. *Courtesy of Toyrareum Collectible Toys.*

This board game's based on the 1970s animated *Addams Family* cartoon. $25-30. *Courtesy of Play With This.*

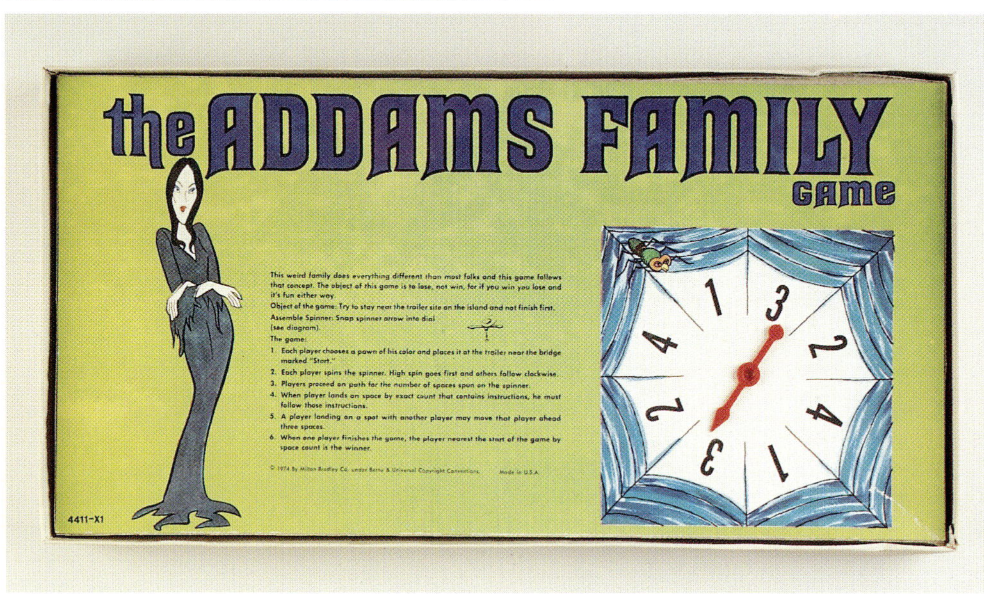

I like the spider web spinner. *Courtesy of Play With This.*

Another monstrous 1970s 'toon was *Groovie Ghoulies*. The game is $20-25. C'mon everybody shout! *Courtesy of Play With This.*

And speaking of spooky families, who can ever forget Barnabas and the clan from Collinswood? Here's the *Dark Shadows* game from the 1960s. $30-40. *Courtesy of Toyrareum Collectible Toys.*

The game board was extra-large and made from heavy-stock paper.

A detail shows a mad dog—always a welcome sight! *Courtesy of Toyrareum Collectible Toys.*

The Barnabas Collins game didn't have much to do with *Dark Shadows* ...

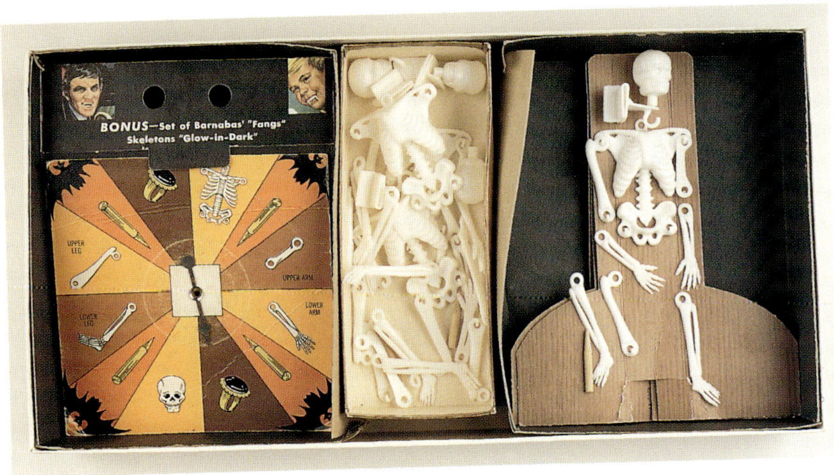

... but it sure had cool skeletons. (Fangs are missing, as usual!) $40-50 complete. *Courtesy of Timmy's Toy Dungeon, Inc.*

Doctor Who was a tremendous source of monsters, but it was mostly the Daleks that were made into toys. Here's a Dapol reissue of a Louis Marx Dalek with pull-back action, approximately 6" tall. Loose $25-30, boxed $60-70. The original's worth three times as much. *Courtesy of Paul Levitt.*

EX-TER-MI-NATE! yells this 1980s Dalek pencil case. $20-25. *Courtesy of Paul Levitt.*

The inflatable Godzilla was first issued by Imperial in the mid-1980s. $20-25. *Courtesy of Paul Levitt.*

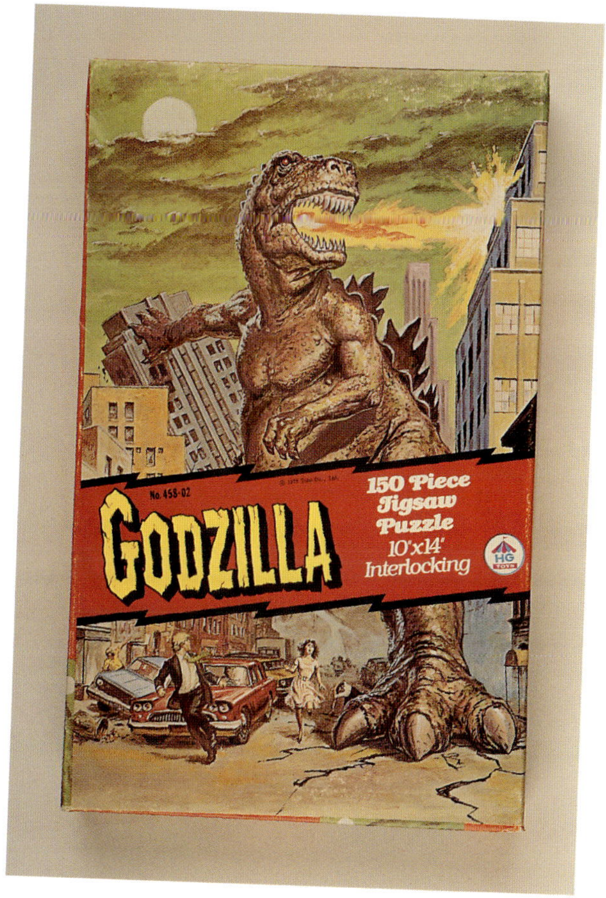

I like the moon. $30-40. *Courtesy of Paul Levitt.*

American issue Godzilla puzzle (at least he's not green) from the 1970s. $30-40. *Courtesy of Paul Levitt.*

In some ways, Trendmasters was the best thing to happen to Godzilla merchandising in the U.S.A. They bought up the license BEFORE TriStar decided to do the film, and began releasing Godzilla toys to an eager new generation. Here's their battery-powered walking Godzilla. $15-20 loose, $30-40 boxed. *Courtesy of Paul Levitt.*

Perhaps their best item is this playset. $25-30 loose and $40-50 boxed. *Courtesy of Paul Levitt.*

The playset included this Godzilla, which fires "atomic breath" missiles from its mouth. *Courtesy of Paul Levitt.*

Trendmasters crafted a near-endless number of Godzilla figures in a bewildering number of types and sizes. Here's a carded bendy. $20-25. *Courtesy of Paul Levitt.*

Here's a Trendmasters windup walker. Loose $4-5. *Courtesy of Paul Levitt.*

We never had Godzilla Shaker Makers in the 1970s but Trendmasters gave us this similar item in the 1990s. $20-25. *Courtesy of Nick Delliponti.*

Walky Sparky Godzilla, 1980s. $15-20. *Courtesy of Paul Levitt.*

This Godzilla Petster rolls around under its own power and responds to sounds. Cute, huh? $40-50 as shown. *Courtesy of Paul Levitt.*

And now a look at four decades of Japan-produced Godzilla merchandise. Bullmark's missile firing Big G was a hit in the early 1970s. Loose $80-90, boxed $150-200. *Courtesy of Paul Levitt.*

Bullmark's vinyl monsters were among the first Godzilla toys. This "standard size" Godzilla (around ten inches tall), originally released in the mid-1960s, is actually a 1990s reissue worth $40-50. *Courtesy of Paul Levitt.*

Yamakatsu also had a run on Godzilla vinyl figures in the early 1980s. $40-50. *Courtesy of Paul Levitt.*

Popy, following after Bullmark and Marusan, was the premiere Godzi-toy maker of the 1970s. $40-50. *Courtesy of Paul Levitt.*

But it was Bandai, beginning in the early 1980s, which has produced the longest-running and most all-encompassing line of vinyl Japanese monsters. Here's their version of Godzilla as he appeared in the mid-1960s. $75-95. *Courtesy of Paul Levitt.*

Superman and Batman should be so heavily merchandised! Godzilla water gun, 1980s. $20-25 as shown. *Courtesy of Paul Levitt.*

Inflatable roly-poly Godzilla, 1980s. $6-8 as shown. *Courtesy of Paul Levitt.*

Light-up Godzilla made by Beetland, approximately 13" high. $150-200 as shown. *Courtesy of Paul Levitt.*

This Godzilla has a super-sticky tongue! $20-25. *Courtesy of Paul Levitt.*

Characon produced this remote control Godzilla in the 1980s. $100-125. *Courtesy of Paul Levitt.*

This red-eyed freak is a Characon knockoff. $40-50. *Courtesy of Paul Levitt.*

Billiken, a maker of toys and models for adult consumers in Japan, has always capitalized on nostalgia. Here's their old-fashioned windup Gojira, made in the 1990s. $80-90. *Courtesy of Paul Levitt.*

Left:
The Japanese love cartoony (or "super deformed") versions of their monsters, and Godzilla is no exception. $8-10 as shown. *Courtesy of Paul Levitt.*

For some reason, they also made a brown one. $30-40 loose. *Courtesy of Paul Levitt.*

This windup egg hatches a Godzilla who walks around. Loose $12-15, MIP $20-25. *Courtesy of Paul Levitt.*

This squeaking bop hammer is a perennial favorite at carnivals. $12-15. *Courtesy of Paul Levitt.*

The assembled model. *Courtesy of Paul Levitt.*

Many models are more intended for grown-ups than kids, like this fancy one based on Big G as seen in *Godzilla vs. Biollante*. $70-80. *Courtesy of Paul Levitt.*

Tricky-action Godzilla games and figures abound in Japan, and they always have great box art. $60-70. *Courtesy of Paul Levitt.*

The Son of Godzilla, Minya (or Minira or Minilla or Milli Vanilli) surrounded by two Gimantises (or Kamakiras). These Bandai figures rate about $20-25 each. *Courtesy of Paul Levitt.*

One of the most popular and sought-after Bandai Godzilla vinyls is the 1963-style Godzilla made in the mid-1980s ($100-125). It took them nearly a decade to make a 1963 Kong ($30-40) so you could reenact *King Kong vs. Godzilla*. *Courtesy of Paul Levitt.*

Below:
This is my favorite Bandai vinyl: the original Ghidrah (or King Ghidorah). Released in the mid-1980s, it was higher priced than most (around $30). Now Ghidrah rates five times that much. It stands about 11 inches tall. *Courtesy of Paul Levitt.*

A darker, brooding baby G for the 1990s, from *Godzilla vs. Mecha Godzilla*. Bandai, $20-25. *Courtesy of Paul Levitt.*

This Ghidrah model from the late 1980s makes for one of the most beautiful and accurate representations of the character. $40-50. *Courtesy of Paul Levitt.*

This pre-Bandai, post-Bullmark Ghidrah has some goofy heads and stands about 5" tall. $50-60. *Courtesy of Paul Levitt.*

The great thing about Bullmark's monster figures from the 1960s is that, although they resemble the characters, they also LOOK like TOYS. This Ghidrah's a good example of Bullmarkian design work, even though it's actually a Bandai reissue worth $50-60. The original, easily, is worth five or six times that. *Courtesy of Paul Levitt.*

The ferocious Ghidrah was not spared the cartoony treatment. Here's a friction-drive model from the early 1980s, complete with mini-Rodan. $25-30. *Courtesy of Paul Levitt.*

Ghidrah returned to movie screens after a fifteen-year absence in the 1991 release *Godzilla vs. King Ghidorah*, looking similar enough that Bandai basically just altered the heads on their figure of the old Ghidrah. $50-60. *Courtesy of Paul Levitt.*

Trendmasters' roaring Ghidrah is proportioned funny (lookit dem lil legs!) but very striking overall. $15-20 loose. $30-35 MIP. *Courtesy of Paul Levitt.*

This stuffed Ghidrah is another squeak hammer. $20-25. *Courtesy of Paul Levitt.*

Godzilla's controversially-campy foes from the mid-1970s, Megalon ($40-50) (or Megaro) and Gigan ($25-30), here vinylized by Bandai. *Courtesy of Paul Levitt.*

An American Ghidrah, this Trendmasters bendy works great with those three necks. Loose $10-12. MIP $20-25. *Courtesy of Paul Levitt.*

The same, as Bullmark reissues by Bandai, each worth $50-60. *Courtesy of Paul Levitt.*

Rodan, the giant Pteranodon, rendered here in Bullmark style. This is a Bandai reissue, worth $50-60. *Courtesy of Paul Levitt.*

Probably the most popular Japanese monster item ever produced in America, the Rodan from the Shogun Warriors line by Mattel. Unlike their Godzilla, this looks VERY much like the actual character. Loose $100-150. Boxed $400-450. *Courtesy of Paul Levitt.*

Rodan didn't escape the whole "super deformed" bit. This toy is an egg that transforms into a pot-bellied Rodan. $20-30. *Courtesy of Paul Levitt.*

This Rodan is one of Bandai's best vinyls. My parents, by the way, saw the original film on a date in 1957. $50-60. *Courtesy of Paul Levitt.*

The dark, brooding Rodan of the 1990s, as seen in *Godzilla vs. Mecha Godzilla* (1993). $25-30. *Courtesy of Paul Levitt.*

And speaking of Mecha Godzilla, here's the evil original from the 1970s films, as crafted by Bandai in the early 1990s. $50-60. *Courtesy of Paul Levitt.*

Here's a vintage Mecchy toy: Characon's remote control Mecha Godzilla. $150-200. *Courtesy of Play With This.*

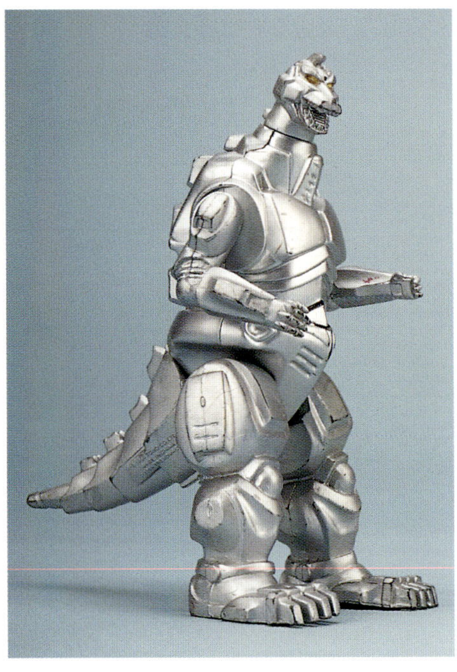

When Trendmasters brought out Mecha Godzilla figures in America, they chose the 1990s design, which few people in America had seen. Here's the 5" action figure. $4-5 loose, $12-15 MIP. *Courtesy of Elisabeth Maria Delliponti.*

Trendmasters made an attractive series of 10" tall figures that made noise endlessly in store shelves. They had proximity detectors and would scream out whenever someone walked past. Even I, seasoned pro that I am, have been caught off guard by a row of tittering Trendmasters Toho terrors from time to time. Loose $6-8. MIP $20-25. *Courtesy of Paul Levitt.*

After the lukewarm return of Godzilla to movie theaters in 1984/85, Toho pulled out all the stops and crafted a big-budget film that adults could sit through along with their kids, just like in the old days. The result was *Godzilla vs. Biollante*. Here's the box for Bandai's Biollante ...

... and the actual figure, pricey when new, and now commanding $300-400 boxed and about half that loose. The film, originally, was to include a second hybrid monster, part rat, part fish, which was cut for budgetary reasons. *Courtesy of Paul Levitt.*

The arch-enemy of the original evil Mecha Godzilla, here's that justly under used cocker spaniel monster King Seesar by Bandai. $20-25. *Courtesy of Paul Levitt.*

Trendmasters was notorious for "adapting" characters they chose to market in the USA. Here, the plant-like Biollante is given big, clawed feet. I dunno, I kinda like them. Loose 6" figure $6-8. MIP $12-15. *Courtesy of Paul Levitt.*

Bandai's version of Mecha Kong ($40-50) battles the other baddie from *King Kong Escapes*, Gorosaurus ($60-70). *Courtesy of Paul Levitt.*

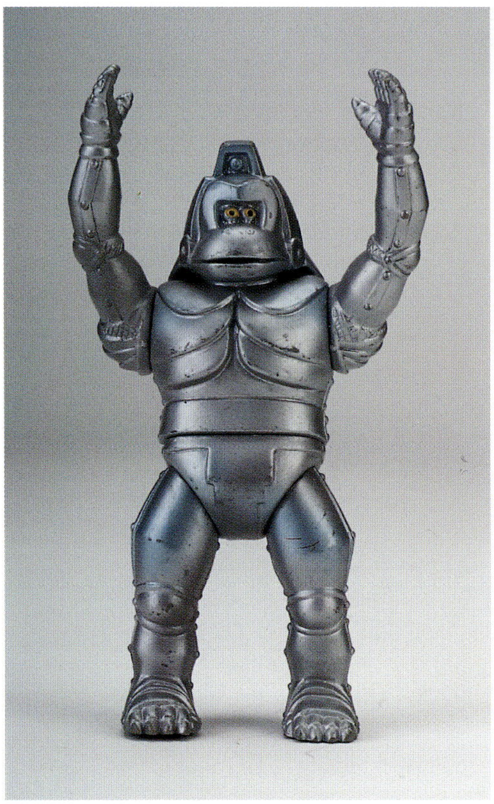

Going further back in time, here's the robot Kong from Toho's *King Kong Escapes*, as crafted by Yamakatsu in the early 1980s. $30-40. *Courtesy of Paul Levitt.*

This detailed figure of Baragon from Toho's *Frankenstein Conquers the World* is one of the most sought-after Bandai vinyls. $200-250. *Courtesy of Paul Levitt.*

You're expecting me to say this is a Bandai reissue of a Bullmark Baragon, but it isn't, It's an ORIGINAL Bullmark Baragon! This one is larger than standard size, standing about 13" tall. These rarely turn up, but $500-600 is not a bad ballpark figure. *Courtesy of Paul Levitt.*

This Yamakatsu Angilas from the early 1980s is favored by Paul Levitt because of its "stoned" expression. $40-50.

Here's Bandai's outstanding Angilas. Flip the tail around and use him as a hair brush (Paul's gag). $50-60. *Courtesy of Paul Levitt.*

Now, these ARE Bandai repros of the Bullmark standard size versions of Baragon (of virtue) and Angilas (or Anguiras). $50-60 each, respectively. *Courtesy of Paul Levitt.*

Bandai's replica of the Mogera (or Moguera) robot from *The Mysterians*. Originally Mogera was to have been a flesh-and-blood monster that burrowed underground. This idea was used instead for Baragon a few movies later. $25-30. *Courtesy of Play With This.*

You didn't think we'd forget HER, did you? This beautiful Mothra was issued by Bandai for *Godzilla vs. Mothra* in 1992. It has translucent plastic wings. Loose $20-30. Boxed $60-75. *Courtesy of Paul Levitt.*

The wings were beautifully done. *Courtesy of Paul Levitt.*

This Mothra wound up as a joint Popy/Bandai product as Bandai took over the Toho monster market in the mid-1980s. Originally issued in a box (and worth $300-400), this more common version from 1991 rates $40-50. Note it has a tag, like almost all Bandai monsters come with when new. *Courtesy of Paul Levitt.*

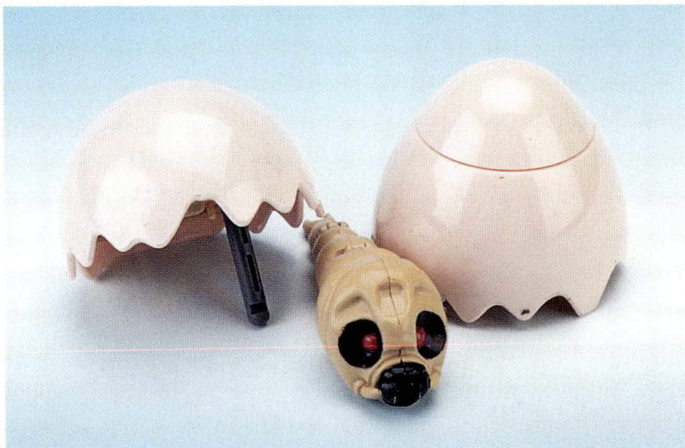

My favorite Mothra larva toy is the windup egg that breaks open and a little windup Mothra crawls out. Loose $10-15, MIP $25-30. *Courtesy of Paul Levitt.*

Trendmasters released a very good 10" Mothra with light up eyes and chirping sound ...

... but its wings were solid plastic and only painted on the top. Loose $10-12. MIP $20-25. *Courtesy of Paul Levitt.*

Bandai's classic-style Mothra larva ($70-80) and 1990s version ($20-25). *Courtesy of Paul Levitt.*

Bandai also reissued Bullmark's standard-size Mothra adult. $50-60. *Courtesy of Paul Levitt.*

A new monster, introduced in *Godzilla vs. Mothra* (1992), was Battra—the "Battle Mothra"—a spirit of vengeance created by the Earth itself. Here he is in caterpillar form from Bandai. $30-40. *Courtesy of Paul Levitt.*

Here's the deluxe Battra. The translucent-wing Mothra you saw earlier came in similar packaging. Loose $20-25. MIP $50-60. *Courtesy of Paul Levitt.*

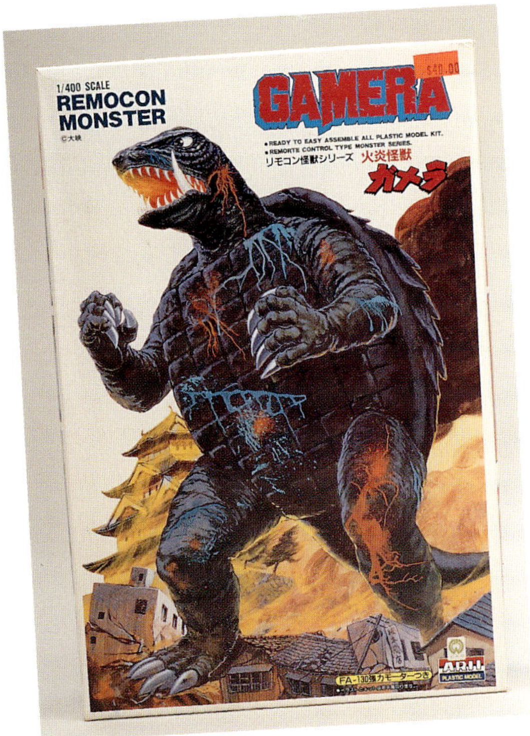

"Gam-ruh!" Neer neer neer neer "Gam-ruh!" And so goes the music you can only hear on the Americanized version of the film *Gammera the Invincible*, the version with Brian Donlevy. Anyway, this motorized kit was widely available in American hobby shops in the 1990s, and is a reissue of an earlier kit. $40-50. *Courtesy of Play With This.*

Bandai's classic vinyl 8" Gamera, $25-30. The version of the first film that is available on tape is the "international" version. That's a version of a film which is dubbed in a kind of rough-draft English to help sell the film to American producers. *Courtesy of Paul Levitt.*

Here's another one of those cool transforming egg figures. $20-30. *Courtesy of Paul Levitt.*

Remember Battling Tops? They're back. In Gamera form. And Gaos form, too. $40-50. *Courtesy of Paul Levitt.*

This dogfight, showing actual shots of Gamera and Gaos, decorates the box lid of a motorized Gaos model kit. $30-40. *Courtesy of Play With This.*

And here he is, Gaos, the arch-enemy of Gamera, as seen in *Return of the Giant Monsters*. (The "international" version, *Gamera vs. Gaos*, is available on video). Bandai 8" series. $25-30. *Courtesy of Paul Levitt.*

Gaos returned with Gamera in the 1995 film known in America as *Gamera Guardian of the Universe*. Here's the dark, brooding 1990s version of Gaos. 3" figure, Bandai, $15-20. *Courtesy of Play With This.*

Here are Bandai's vinyl versions of Gamera's foes Barugon (*War of the Monsters*) and Jiger (*Gamera vs. Monster X*). Each rates $25-30. *Courtesy of Paul Levitt.*

It's curious how these reissues of rare motorized kits were widely available in American hobby shops in the 1990s. The line also includes Gappa from *Monster from a Prehistoric Planet*. $30-40. *Courtesy of Paul Levitt.*

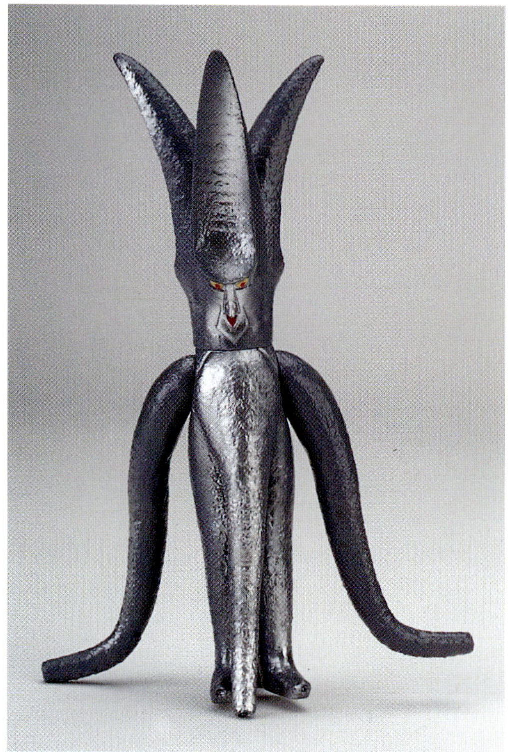

My favorite Gamera foe, Viras, from *Destroy All Planets*. Bandai's outstanding version (8" series) is $25-30. *Courtesy of Paul Levitt.*

Guiron, a real cut-up, battled both Gaos and Gamera in *Attack of The Monsters* (international English version is titled *Gamera vs. Guiron*). *Courtesy of Paul Levitt.*

The mid-1990s saw a great invention by Bandai. Motorized walking robots who wore rubber monster suits just like the actors! Here's the Gamera version.

Zigra, Gamera's last 1970s foe, never saw his movie get an official American release back in those days, so the only English version we can see is the international dub known as *Gamera vs. Zigra*. $20-25. *Courtesy of Paul Levitt.*

The robot mechanism is in the center, with the shell on the right and the suit on the left. $95-125. *Courtesy of Play With This.*

Gamera returned in 1997 in *Gamera 2*, and this transforming figure shows off his new ability.

You can make a regular Gamera about 11" tall ...

... or a flying Gamera, by switching his feet for fins! $100-125. *Courtesy of Play With This.*

Finally, here's my favorite walking Gamera toy, from the 1995 film ...

ROOOAAARRR!!!! $100-125. *Courtesy of Play With This.*

Chapter 4. JAPANESE TV MONSTERS

There are very few things in this world I really care about, but four of the things I do care about are *Ultraman, The Space Giants, Johnny Sokko*, and *Spectreman*.

Ultraman is the best-known Japanese character in the world after Godzilla. His various TV programs have aired in almost every country and many are still being broadcast today.

Ultraman, for you sad individuals who don't know, is the creation of Eiji Tsuburaya, the special effects wizard behind the early Godzilla films. Growing restless in the mid-1960s, he established Tsuburaya Enterprises and began making TV shows. His first production ultimately became known as *Ultra Q*. The "Q" stood for the unknown, much like Star Trek's precious villain, and the "Ultra", well, it just sounded cool.

Ultra Q was a cross between *The Outer Limits* and *The X-Files*, in which our pilot hero and his sidekicks would encounter mysterious forces that usually led to an alien invasion threat or a giant monster. Then, the authorities would deal with it—if they could. Kenji Sahara, star of Toho's *Rodan*, played the hero.

This grew into a new program in which a giant robotic hero would battle the monsters—who would then have to pick on somebody their own size. This became *Ultraman*, a 39-episode series of half-hour shows. The Science Patrol, (Hiyata, Ito, Arashi, Captain Mura, and Fuji) would use their arsenal of super-weapons against marauding giant monsters, but it was only when Hiyata became Ultraman that the good guys were able to win. To bless the show, several elements from *Ultra Q* were brought in. Hiroko Sakurai, the female lead in *Ultra Q*, played Fuji. Almost everyone in the cast of *Ultraman* had played guest parts in *Ultra Q*. And several of the "Q" monsters returned as well.

When merchandise for *Ultraman* began, in fact, the monsters that were used were often *Ultra Q* beasts, whether they appeared on *Ultraman* or not.

On the few, rare examples of American *Ultraman* merchandise, for example, the monsters depicted are mostly *Ultra Q* monsters. The rare *Ultraman* model kit line featured American releases of Aurora-like models of Ultraman, Pegila and Pagos, and you guessed it, Pegila and Pagos were actually *Ultra Q* monsters. Pagos is also featured on the American Ultraman Halloween costume, but the most prominent monster pictured on it is Red King, a REAL Ultra-foe.

Ultraman inspired an endless (so far) series of sequel shows that have aired in Japan and in most other areas of the world, but rarely in America, and never with the lasting impact that the original had on kids of the 1960s and 1970s. This book will just focus on toys based on the original, much-loved *Ultraman* series that aired in syndication here in English.

At exactly the same time that *Ultraman* was being produced, a live-action version of famed cartoonist Osamu Tezuka's comic strip *Magma Taishi* was also being filmed. It beat *Ultraman* to the air by one week in Japan. (Both aired in the Summer of 1966.)

Eventually it was dubbed into English and went through several name changes, including *Space Avenger* and *Monsters from Outer Space*. But the name under which it is best known in the United States is *The Space Giants*.

Before you read any further, you need to understand that *The Space Giants* is not just my favorite TV show, not just my favorite thing from my childhood, not just my favorite entertainment. *The Space Giants* is my absolute favorite THING in the world. I like it better than G.I. Joe, the Impressionists, Devil Dogs, girls, the Ramones, fresh air, Univision, cats, or dogs. It means more to me than any person, object, event, or knowledge that I have already, or that I may one day, experience, posses, or enjoy throughout my lifetime.

And I can say that with total conviction because in my heart I know it's true.

I can't remember the first time I saw *The Space Giants*. It was just always there, from the very beginning of my memory.

The Space Giants is the story of Rodak, an evil mastermind from the far planet of Makah, who covets the earth because it is the most beautiful planet he has ever seen. His hobby is collecting planets, but the others he's conquered are barren and ugly. The Earth must be added to his collection.

Fortunately for us, he has been trailed to Earth by the wise wizard Methusem, who is aided by a giant robot named Goldar and his human-sized wife, Silvar. Goldar befriends young Miko Mura, son of wire service reporter Ito "Tom" Mura, and together this band of humans and robots thwarts thirteen consecutive plots laid by Rodak over a span of fifty-two half-hour episodes.

Sadly, *The Space Giants*, when viewed overall, is unremarkable in many ways, especially compared to *Ultraman*.

Whereas *Ultraman* would face at least one new monster every episode, monsters were stretched from two to four episodes apiece in *The Space Giants*. The effects were hurriedly executed and not at all convincing, although many of the animated effects are passable and Rodak's bat-shaped space ship is always impressive to see.

The dialogue is absolutely awful. A typical conversation in Space Giants-ese goes like this: PERSON #1: "I believe Rodak is the cause of the strange events that have been happening recently." PERSON #2: "I also am of that opinion. I also believe this opinion of ours will soon turn out to be fact."

However, all of this can be forgiven because of Rodak himself. He is the ultimate TV villain. He is hampered in no way by any feelings of guilt or remorse over his actions. In fact, he sees the damage he inflicts on the Earthlings as punishment for their not surrendering sooner. During one tense moment when he is awaiting a response to his latest ultimatum, Rodak muses, "Why do the Earthlings force me to do this to them?"

Rodak has all the best dialogue because his face is a mask that does not allow much mouth movement. Therefore it isn't necessary to mangle sentences to fit his lips movements, as it is with Ito Mura and the gang, who drone on endlessly. Very often, when there's nothing important for Rodak to say, the dialogue writers just have him laugh. And laugh. And why not? He was usually pretty happy. He totally outmatched Goldar, who was a stiff, even for a robot. Goldar was constantly swearing to destroy Rodak, and yet Rodak routinely won little victories over him. "I will find Rodak and make him pay," Goldar would say, shaking his fist. *The Space Giants* is the only TV show in history where the hero makes more empty threats than the villain.

In fact, and not to give away the ending, the only reason Rodak is finally defeated is that toward the end of the series he gets very anxious about his losses and gambles on one last, particularly risky and foolish endeavor. If he had just bided his time, he might be plotting against Earth to this very day.

Like *Ultraman*, *The Space Giants* has its share of famous monsters. Original vintage SG toys were not marketed in America and most vintage items do not exist anywhere outside of Japan. We do have some, though, plus some relatively recent items aimed at Japanese and Americans who have mourned the lack of Space Giants toys in the last two decades or so.

Ultraman and *The Space Giants* started a giant monster phase on Japanese TV. Shows that followed, like *Captain Ultra* and *Monster Prince*, featured giant monsters, while 1970s epics like *Kikaider* and *Kamen Rider* carried the robotic super hero concept to new levels.

One other 1960s-era giant monster show had a long life in syndication in America, and it is probably better-known than *The Space Giants*. It's called *Johnny Sokko And His Flying Robot*.

Even by the standards of other giant monster shows, JSAHFR is pretty ridiculous. It has incredibly tacky special effects and especially outlandish plots and monsters. It can be said reasonably that where you might laugh along with *Ultraman* or *The Space Giants*, you're more likely to laugh at *Johnny Sokko*.

Which is not to say that *Johnny Sokko* is a bad show, or that it is not entertaining. In fact, it is EXTREMELY entertaining. Its mile-a-minute pacing blows away the lethargy of a typical *Space Giants* story. Its endless parade of kooky characters makes the *Ultraman* gang look bland by comparison. Plus JSAHFR incorporates a "James Bondian" premise into the proceedings.

Whereas *Ultraman* has no overall villain, and *The Space Giants* merely had Rodak and his spaceship gang, the villains in *Johnny Sokko* spring from an extensive paramilitary organization based worldwide and blessed with enough weapons, vehicles, and spy gadgets to keep any good guy at bay. This dark organization was the "Gargoyle Gang," a group of human terrorists organized by Emperor Guillotine, an alien from the planet Gargoyle who looked like a man wearing an octopus over his head.

Guillotine employed a series of lieutenants from all over the universe to aid him in his schemes. There was Doctor Botanus, the chrome-domed, silver-faced scientist and expert on the Gargoyle Vine. And how about Fangar, with his high forehead and machine-gun peg leg? Or Harlequin, the eye patched mastermind whose costume was covered in black diamond designs?

Opposing them was Unicorn, the international organization of lame secret agents who dressed in simply fabulous gold and red uniforms, topped off with ascots. They were only too happy to recruit a young boy named Johnny Sokko into their ranks when the preteen accidentally gained control of the Gargoyle Gang's secret weapon—a giant robot. Obeying only Johnny's commands, the Robot was enlisted in service to Unicorn.

Although it only ran 26 episodes, *Johnny Sokko and His Flying Robot* was a perennial favorite in afternoon syndication on UHF channels like Philly 17, The Great Entertainer. No toys were ever released in America, and even today very few have been issued for the nostalgia crowd, even in Japan. However, in the 1990s, we have been given the put-together action figures of Giant Robot and Torozon, plus a windup walking Giant Robot, and a few Marmit vinyl figure creations including the Robot, Torozon (GR2) Skallion and Dracolon.

The final member of this fantastic foursome of nostalgic giant monster shows is a series that slipped through the cracks in American TV, but was glimpsed by a lucky few while it was on in the late 1970s. This was *Spectreman*, a popular *Ultraman* knock-off produced in the 1970s by the people who made *The Space Giants*.

Spectreman was a cyborg from space who was sent to the Earth to battle the evil space apeman Dr. Gori and his

Beetland Ultraman lighter. $20-20. *Courtesy of Paul Levitt.*

Here's a super deformed giant piggy bank, standing about 13 inches. $40-50. Boxed $90-100. *Courtesy of Paul Levitt.*

This is a more budget-minded mask, but still not bad. 1990s. $30-40. MIP $80-90. *Courtesy of Paul Levitt.*

One of Bandai's earliest Ultraman toys is this bendy which stands about 7 inches tall. $40-50. *Courtesy of Paul Levitt.*

Windup walking Ultraman, 1980s. $15-20. *Courtesy of Paul Levitt.*

The 1990s saw Ultraman figures in all types and size ranges. $40-50. *Courtesy of Paul Levitt.*

Stuffed Ultraman with race car, approximately 8" tall, 1990s. $20-30. *Courtesy of Paul Levitt.*

This flying Ultraman had a battery-operated propeller that allowed him to fly in a circle on a string. $70-80. *Courtesy of Paul Levitt.*

One of the best, yet affordable, Ultraman toys from recent years is a series of models that includes this one. Box size is roughly six by four inches. $20-25. *Courtesy of Paul Levitt.*

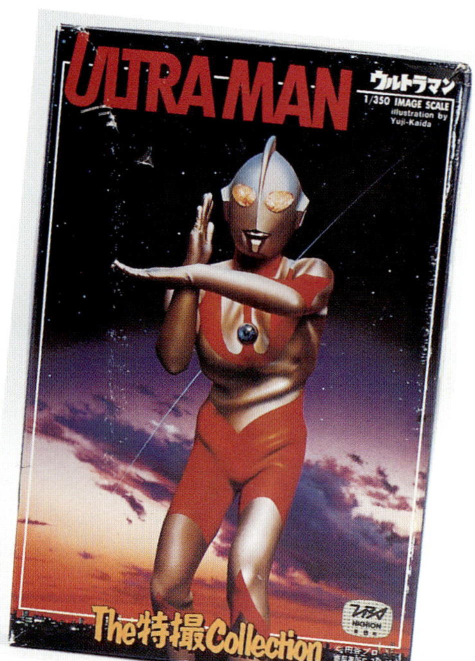

Like all good, heavily-merchandised super heroes, Ultraman can be found all around the house. Soap Dish $30-40. *Courtesy of Paul Levitt.*

Ultraman Water Gun. $20-25. *Courtesy of Paul Levitt.*

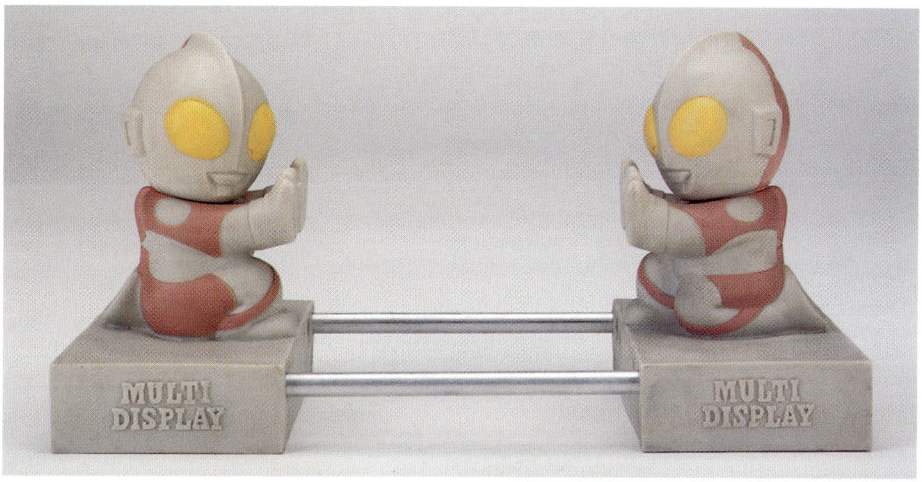

Another household helper is the Ultraman CD rack, for all your Kome Kome Club and Shonen Knife CDs. $30-40. *Courtesy of Paul Levitt.*

Ultraman's a venerable character and his 25th anniversary in 1991 was cause to celebrate! Sticker $12-15. *Courtesy of Paul Levitt.*

Reissues and similarly-styled reintroductions make for affordable versions of classic toys. This 1990s Ultraman windup robot will set you back $125-150 boxed, whereas an original would cost you twenty times as much. *Courtesy of Paul Levitt.*

This is a Bullmark EVIL Ultraman (actually Zarob in disguise) who appeared in an original episode. $50-60. MIP $100-125. And thus we introduce the ENEMIES OF ULTRAMAN! *Courtesy of Paul Levitt.*

The evil Baltans first appeared in the second episode of *Ultraman*. Here, a two-foot-tall specimen battles a giant Ultraman, both courtesy of Bandai and both $150-200 loose and $250-300 boxed. *Courtesy of Paul Levitt.*

Baltan and Ultraman finger puppets, 1990s. $4-5. *Courtesy of Paul Levitt.*

Hanging stuffy Baltan, 1990s, $12-15. *Courtesy of Paul Levitt.*

Roly-sparky Baltan and windup-walky Batlan, each $12-15.
Courtesy of Paul Levitt.

Windup walking Baltan mini-model, 1980s. $30-40. *Courtesy of Paul Levitt.*

This meditating Baltan uses the popular "locust" position to contemplate his abdomen. Vinyl bank, 1990s. $30-40. *Courtesy of Paul Levitt.*

Novelty Baltan with light-up eyes, 1990s. $30-40. *Courtesy of Paul Levitt.*

This rubberized Baltan model (1980s) is a companion piece to the Ultraman kit that opens this chapter. $80-90. *Courtesy of Paul Levitt.*

Likewise, this bendy Bandai Baltan is from the same line as the earlier Ultraman. $50-60. *Courtesy of Paul Levitt.*

The Baltans did not escape the popular egg monsters line! $25-30. *Courtesy of Paul Levitt.*

Baltan Lighter by Beetland. $30-40. *Courtesy of Paul Levitt.*

Baltan Mascot Winkers wired into your brake lights. It's Rumba time! Bal-tan Mas-cot Win-ker! You get no friends with sa-lad! $30-40. *Courtesy of Paul Levitt.*

Economy brand Baltan mask. 1990s. $20-30. *Courtesy of Paul Levitt.*

Large 13" vinyl Baltan, Bandai, mid-1980s. *Courtesy of Paul Levitt.*

Baltan's father? Just about! This "cicadaman" appeared on *Ultra Q* before the Baltans were introduced on *Ultraman*. 1970s vinyl, 10" tall. $70-80. MIP $100-125.

Starting in the early 1980s, Bandai began issuing *Ultraman* monsters and heroes as 6" vinyl figures. Here are the original versions of Baltan ($20-25), Da Da ($12-15) and Z-Ton ($15-18). *Courtesy of Paul Levitt.*

Repainted Baltan ($12-15), original Mefilas ($15-18) and Mecha Baltan, who is from the Andro Melos series which was set in the Ultra universe ($12-15). *Courtesy of Paul Levitt.*

Mefilas, as the only alien to beat Ultraman to a draw, is a popular figure with toy and model companies. Vinyl kit, $60-70. *Courtesy of Paul Levitt.*

And Space Dinosaur Z-Ton, the only monster who ever BEAT Ultraman, is immortalized in this economy model kit. $20-25. *Courtesy of Paul Levitt.*

Here's an early Bandai bendy Z-ton, $50-60. *Courtesy of Paul Levitt.*

Batman and Robin (or reasonable facsimiles) join the members of Ultraman's Science Patrol (or reasonable facsimiles) in this puzzle set. $100-125. *Courtesy of Paul Levitt.*

Ultraman battles Gyango. $20-25. *Courtesy of Paul Levitt.*

Bemlar and Gabadon go at it. $20-25. *Courtesy of Paul Levitt.*

Right:
The Science Patrol, Johnny Sokko, and Miko from *The Space Giants* face Ultraman monster Antlar as Baltan looks on contentedly. $20-25. *Courtesy of Paul Levitt.*

I never realized that Aboras was made from an old Red King suit until I held the two Bandai figures side by side. Bandai's Aboras figure is a copy of their Red King figure from the neck down. $15-20. *Courtesy of Paul Levitt.*

This Pigmon hand puppet (1990s) looks ashamed. But he is friendly to mankind. He's a very small monster, isn't that right? $20-30. *Courtesy of Paul Levitt.*

More Bandai 6" vinyls, Guezra, Gyango, and Skydon, each $12-15. *Courtesy of Paul Levitt.*

Siboz, the monster who just wanted to go home to the Ultra Zone, is shown in alternate baggie packaging. $15-20. *Courtesy of Paul Levitt.*

Gubira (the drill fish) and Kemler (or Kemura), more 6" vinyls. $12-15 each. *Courtesy of Paul Levitt.*

This Telesdon shows off his photo tag. $15-18. *Courtesy of Paul Levitt.*

Neronga, Dorako, and Gohora—except that this "Dorako" is patterned after his second appearance in *Ultraman*, when Geronimon brought him back to life, as opposed to the original Dorako who had a single head spike and blades instead of hands. Got that? Each $12-15. *Courtesy of Paul Levitt.*

Gohora (originally Gomora), as a windup miniature model, enjoys his beautiful box art. $50-60. *Courtesy of Paul Levitt.*

You may have caught *Ultraman: Toward The Future* during its brief syndication run in the US in the early 1990s. It was a 13-episode series produced in Australia. This Playset ($20-30) was produced for the figures. *Courtesy of Paul Levitt.*

Ultra Q's Kemur alien returned as the Z-Ton leader in the final episode of *Ultraman*. Vinyl 1970s figure, 11" tall. $60-70. $150-175 MIP. Courtesy of Paul Levitt.

Right:
The Gerukadon was the smallest creature on the show but the largest figure! Around 9" high. $10-12 loose, $20-25 boxed. *Courtesy of Paul Levitt.*

Australian Ultra-Monsters Barrangas and Majaba, each $10-12 loose, $20-25 boxed. *Courtesy of Paul Levitt.*

It's my book, so I can bend the rules. I said I would stick to only American-seen *Ultraman* characters, but this G.I.Joe-size figure of Hideki Go from *The Return of Ultraman* is just too cool to pass up. Mr. Go was the man who became the revived Ultraman, fighting new versions of Baltan and Z-Ton in 1971. $200-300. *Courtesy of Paul Levitt.*

Aussie Beasts Shilagi and Broads had their names changed to Killazee and Bogun for the packaging. Each $12-15 loose. $20-25 MIP. *Courtesy of Paul Levitt.*

Pegila is one of the *Ultra Q* monsters merchandised with early Ultraman products. Here is the rare American-issue figure kit. Pegila returned as Chandorah to become Red King's first victim. As shown $175-200. Boxed $400-500. *Author's Collection.*

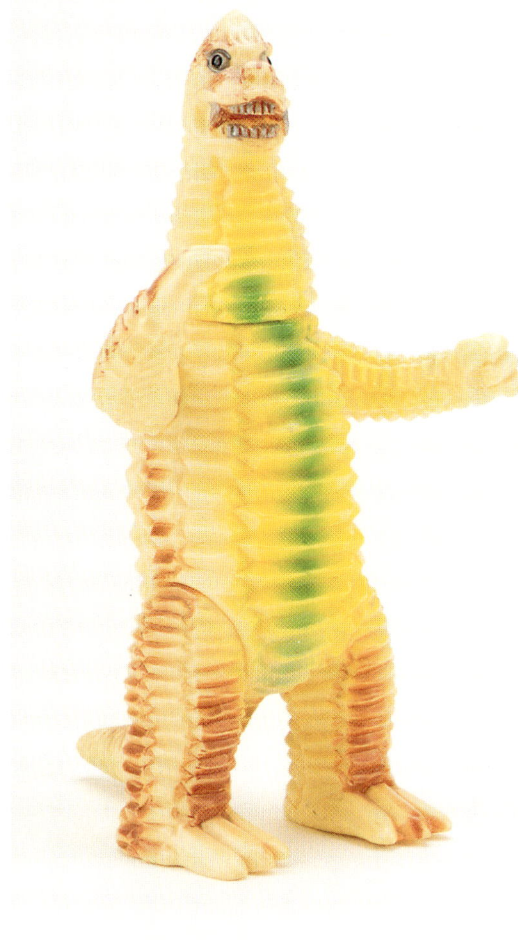

And now, the good stuff. The quintessential Red King collectible, the Bullmark Standard-Size Red King (about 9" tall). Loose $150-200. MIP $350-400. *Author's Collection.*

This Bullmark motorized Red King kit, circa the late 1960s, features the kind of box art that elevates these toys to legendary status. Loose $500-600. Boxed $1000-1200. *Author's Collection.*

This Bandai kit, circa early 1980s, is a reissue of the Bullmark one, in purple plastic. $200-250. *Author's Collection.*

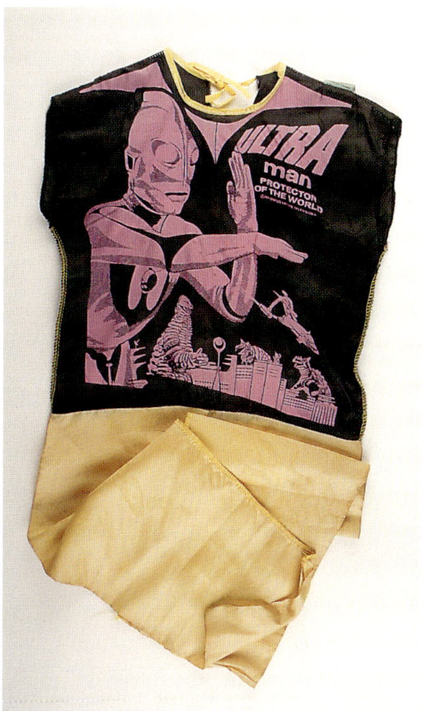

This Collegeville Halloween costume is one of only a handful of known American Ultraman products. Loose (with mask) $100-150. Boxed $250-300. *Author's Collection.*

A detail shot shows Red King prominently. Where are the Baltans? They ain't so hot! *Author's Collection.*

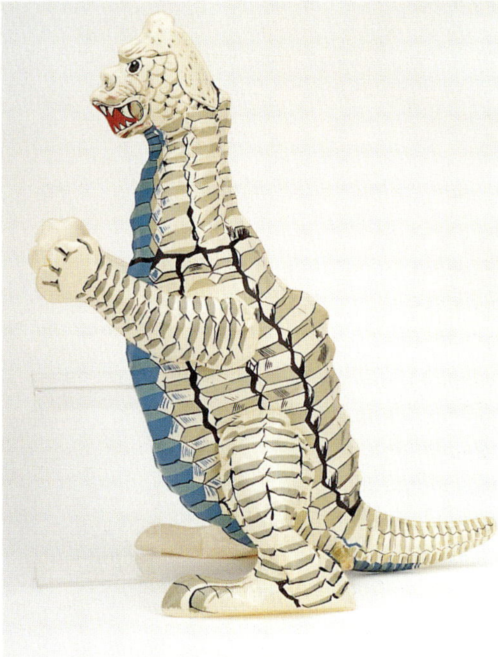

This 1960s Bullmark inflatable Red King once belonged to Damon Foster, publisher of *Oriental Cinema* magazine. I obtained this one to upgrade my own, which had a slow leak. Loose $200-250. MIP $400-500. *Author's Collection.*

This is a finger puppet that came in a three-pack containing Ultraman and the *Return of Ultraman* monster Astoron. Loose $70-80 set. MIP (all three puppets) $200-250. *Author's Collection.*

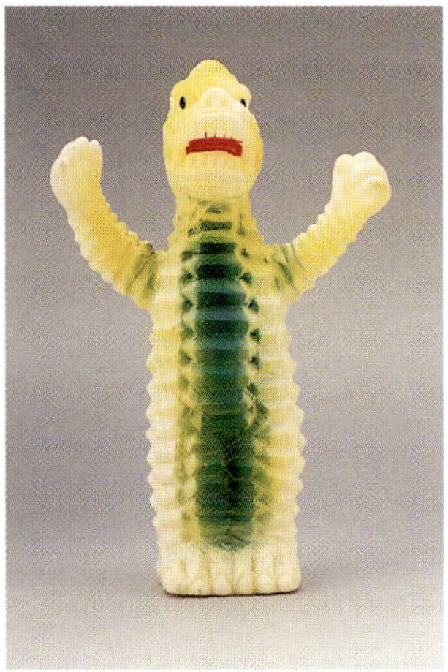

This Giant Red King is a reissue from 1992. Note the color scheme variations. Also, it's lighter in weight. $75-100. *Author's Collection.*

This Bandai Giant Red King from 1984 can be seen on the windowsill in an early scene in the motion picture classic *Pee-Wee's Big Adventure*. $100-150. *Author's Collection.*

Another close-copy remake from Bandai is this doppleganger Bullmark Giant Red King, originally produced in the early 1970s. This repro's worth $200-300, half of the original. The original Tokyo Tower prop had blue paint detailing. *Author's Collection.*

This poseable cardboard Red King dates from the late 1970s, during the poseable cardboard character craze. Loose $70-80. MIP $150-200. *Author's Collection.*

Often, the smaller the Bullmark, the rarer it is. This mini-Red King stands about 5" tall. $150-200. *Author's Collection.*

Oh, now he's just showing off. The Bullmark original in the middle is joined by a 1992 Bandai reissue (gold) ($80-90) and an unlicensed 1980s knockoff (green) ($50-60). *Author's Collection.*

The first time I attended Chiller Theater, I said to my girlfriend, "If I can just find a Billiken Red King, I'm happy." Here it is. Built Up $30-40. MIP $70-80. *Author's Collection.*

This looks like a 10" Popy Red King, but the lack of marking suggests it is a 1980s knockoff. Still, it's worth a good $100-150. And, hey, it's red. *Author's Collection.*

I love to tell visitors that this rubber, wire-armature Red King is a model originally used in designing the original costume, but really it's just a Bandai toy. $60-70. *Author's Collection.*

This gorgeous box art covers a pyramid-shaped windup model kit. $50-60. *Author's Collection.*

The only easily-located Red King toy is the Characon Remote Control RK in mid-1980s packaging. I knocked the eye out of this fellow by running him off a table by accident. I'm gonna love him to death, that boy! $80-100. *Author's Collection.*

This box contains small plastic models of everything you see here. $80-90. *Author's Collection.*

The 1990s have produced some incredible Red King items, like this hand puppet. If anybody knows WHERE the Red King suit pictured on the box is from, contact me at jmars@toyzilla.com. Loose $15-20. MIP $30-40. *Author's Collection.*

As if Red King weren't already a sweetie, here he is in a bag of sweeties. $15-20. *Author's Collection.*

My friend Paul Levitt gathered money from other friends and made a special trip to Yaohan Plaza in North Jersey to get me this singing, rotating alarm clock for my birthday. $150-200. *Author's Collection.*

And here's the Sound Battler version, that roars when you aim a TV remote at it. $80-90. *Author's Collection.*

So Steve Ross calls me up and says, "I know you collect Red King, but do you like cute, cartoony Red Kings? 'Cause there's this bank at the Ultra Plus Gift Shop in San Gabriel..." It roars when you put money in. $150-200. *Author's Collection.*

One nice thing about the Los Angeles-made *Ultraman* series (never shown on American TV) was that it gave us a red Red King. (Well, maroon.) Here's the Bandai figure. $20-25. *Author's Collection.*

I was a guest at ComicFest in 1993, promoting my comic book *Mortar Man*. One or two people cared, but overall it was a letdown. I was extremely pleased to pick up this windup walking RK model, though. $30-40. *Author's Collection.*

When I lived in Southern California, I saw this overpriced pop up book in Little Tokyo, and I promised myself I'd buy it when I sold the 1970s action figure book I'd written. Well, that book is now in stores, and here is this book. Twenty-six bucks! *Author's Collection.*

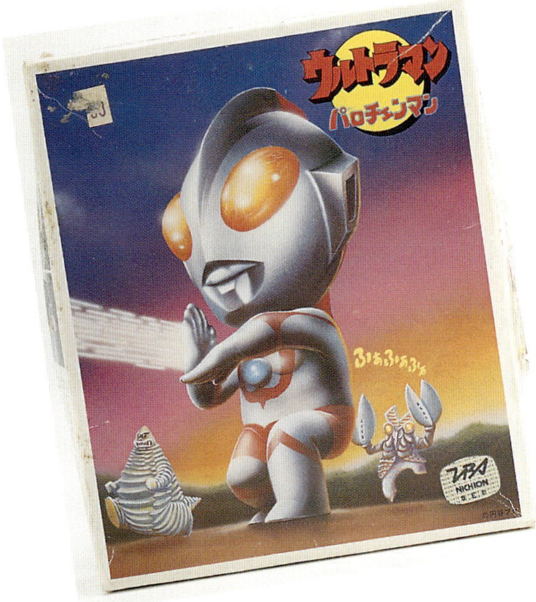

This 1980s friction-powered Ultraman model came with the little tiny Baltan and Red King seen in the corner. So it goes... in my sack. $20-25. *Author's Collection.*

It makes no difference to me whether a Red King item is licensed or not— it's all rare. Steve Ross found this carded set (there's Red King art by Ultraman's upraised hand) for a buck at a tienda mexicana in El Monte, California. $10-12. *Author's Collection.*

Paul Levitt, the F/X Channel's Japanese Monster Maven, is forever breaking up sets of things to give me the Red King out of the set. I salute him—and this Red King pin from a set of Ultra monster pins. $15-20. *Author's Collection.*

Vinyl Claw, approximately 9" tall. $200-250. *Courtesy of Paul Levitt.*

So Paul Levitt and I are at Atlantique City and he's squawking over the price of this Bullmark 1960s Goldar, and I sez ta him I sez, "If you don't buy it, I will." He bought it. $400-500. *Courtesy of Gee I. Wonder.*

I bought this vinyl Magno at a novelty store Heaven in our local mall in 1983. I didn't like the paint so I painted it. $150-200 as is. *Courtesy of Paul Levitt.*

Same goes for this Dillus. $150-200 as shown. *Courtesy of Paul Levitt.*

Billiken Windup Goldar, 1990s. $150-200. *Courtesy of Paul Levitt.*

This is a rare 8" Goldar from the same series. $300-400. *Author's Collection.*

This is the packaging these 8" figures came in. *Courtesy of Paul Levitt.*

This motorized model is one of the few relatively-common *Space Giants* items. $50-60. *Courtesy of Paul Levitt.*

The Space Giants has been an American comic twice, once in the 1970s and then, amazingly enough, in the 1990s. These are the only issues. *Author's Collection.*

Marmit, a Japanese company, produced 1990s figures in the style of the old Bullmark vinyls, specifically aimed at adult collectors. They are new products and run about $50 each. The packaging says "for ages 18 and up" right on it! Here's Moleasaurus ...

... Birdaurus ...

... Zandosus ...

... Taron the Terrible (originally made from the costume of Aron, who starred in his own miniseries) ...

... and Gana, all from *The Space Giants*, and all *Courtesy of Paul Levitt.*

... Renautis and Drox ...

... Vacuma ...

Goldar battles Taron in this unlicensed puzzle. But that's not Birdaurus in the sky— it's Gappa from the movie *Monster From A Prehistoric Planet*! $25-30. *Courtesy of Paul Levitt.*

It's not a toy but it is a sought-after *Space Giants* collectible. This issue of *The Monster Times* features one of the few—maybe the only—articles written on *The Space Giants* when it was in syndication.

Here's the article ...

... and a wacky fumetti featuring the Apollo astronauts and Molesaurus, Renautis, Lodi, and Birdaurus flying past. $100-125. *Author's Collection.*

There were more Johnny Sokko toys made in the 1990s for the nostalgia crowd than there were when the show was new. Here is a you-build-it 12" figure of the Robot, 1990s. $150-200. *Courtesy of Paul Levitt.*

A Spectreman glass from Europe, early 1980s. $15-20. *Courtesy of Paul Levitt.*

This motorized kit is circa 1980 and features the Spectreman monster Magnetron, the mole/catfish. $75-100. *Courtesy of Timmy's Toy Dungeon, Inc.*

And this one features Bakula, the scott-free cyclopean bee. $125-150. *Courtesy of Timmy's Toy Dungeon, Inc.*

Chapter 5. MONSTERS UNLEASHED!

In addition to all the famous monsters of filmland and TV land, there are all those weird, creepy things that turn up in toy stores and on flea market tables that don't easily fit into any one category.

This is a chapter lovingly devoted to those most mysterious of monsters, the ones from the *"What-The -Hell-Is-That?"* school.

One of the founding fathers of this group is Colorforms line of Outer Space Men, a series of bendable characters produced in the 1960s and designed to "go with" Mattel's six-inch Major Matt Mason, a bendable astronaut action figure. A second series of bendies was designed but never sold on the mass market. These characters' images have resurfaced over the years in different forms. The Japanese company Bullmark even made large vinyl figures of the original characters.

Since their debut in the late 1960s, Colorforms repeatedly enlisted both the original seven characters and their second-series brothers to appear on various merchandise throughout the years, as generic "space men." That's why folks like Astro-Nautilus and Colossus Rex appear uncredited on 1970s puzzles to cash in on the "space fever" generated by *Star Wars*. Even in recent years, these popular designs have been recrafted as various figures in generic play sets.

Many other monsters were originated as toys. One of the most visually-arresting lines is Hasbro's Inhumaoids series from the 1980s, of which we have several examples. Other company generated monster lines include Mattel's Rocks 'n Bugs 'n Things and the inhabitants of The Other World by Arco.

And alongside these characters are many strange and unusual ones whose origins can't be traced, because they lead only to the cobwebbed corridors of those people who design gumball machine prizes and other novelties. These monstrosities merely bare the mark "Made in Hong Kong" or "Made in China." I say don't try to understand 'em, just bring 'em out and shoot 'em, with a camera.

So get ready for anything, because you're about to see the wildest collection of bulky, lumbering, google-eyed beasties this side of the Republican National Convention!

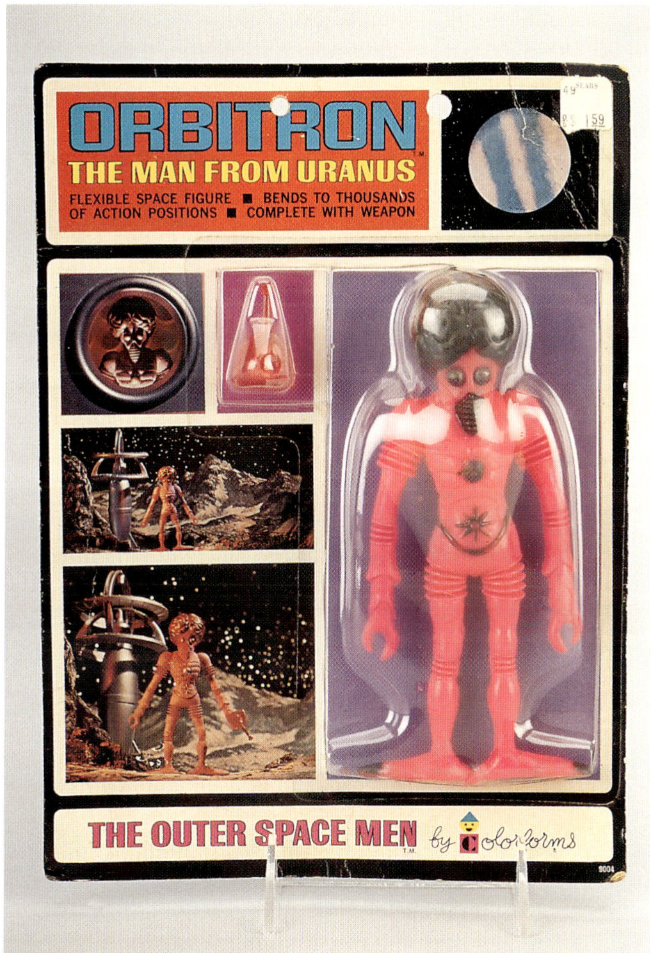

The Colorforms Outer Space Men are perhaps the greatest group of gargoyles created by a toy company. Orbitron's $100-125 loose, $700-800 carded. *Courtesy of Timmy's Toy Dungeon, Inc.*

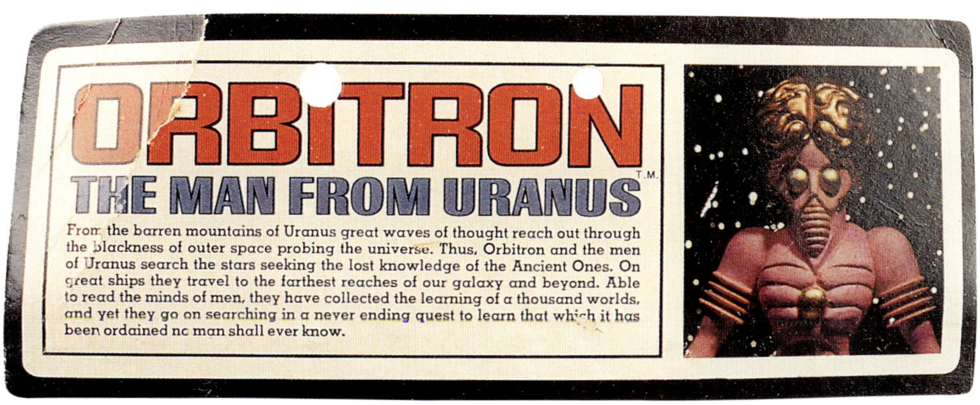

Left:
The Orbitron story, from his card back. *Courtesy of Timmy's Toy Dungeon, Inc.*

Astro-Nautilus is $150-175 loose, $800-900 carded. *Courtesy of Timmy's Toy Dungeon, Inc.*

The Astro-Nautilus story, from his card back. *Courtesy of Timmy's Toy Dungeon, Inc.*

Electron + is $100-125 loose, $700-800 carded. *Courtesy of Timmy's Toy Dungeon, Inc.*

The shocking tale of Electron +, from his card back. *Courtesy of Timmy's Toy Dungeon, Inc.*

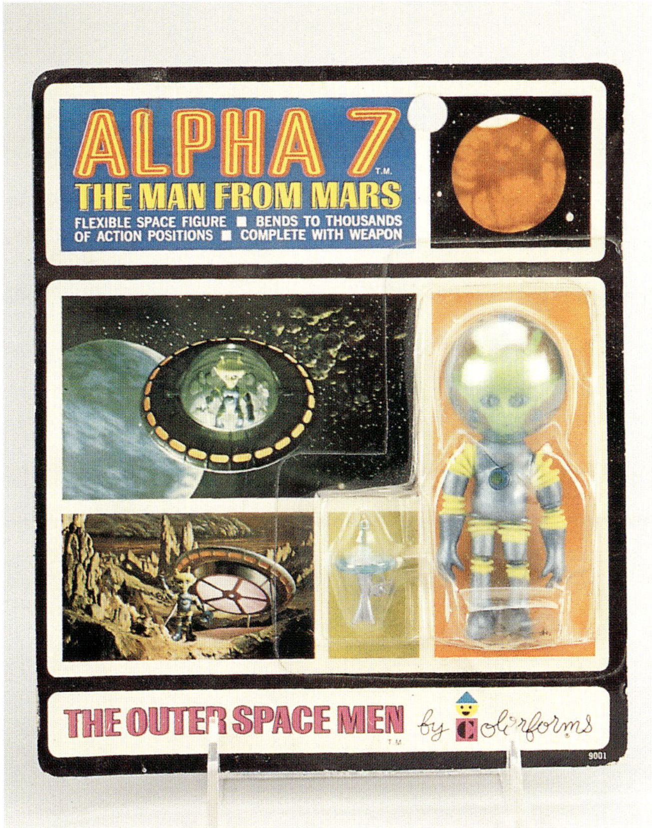

Alpha 7 is $75-95 loose, $500-600 carded. *Courtesy of Timmy's Toy Dungeon, Inc.*

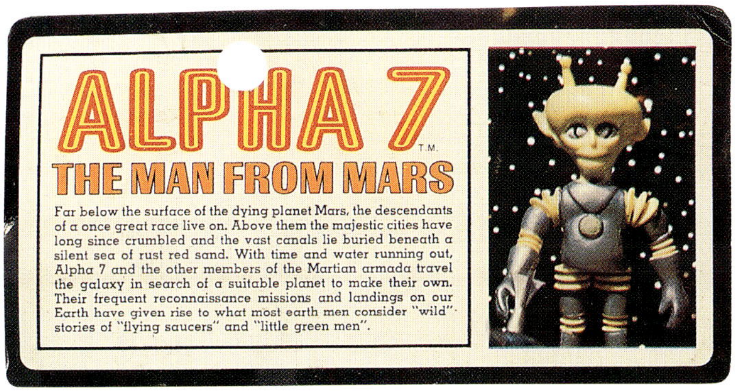

A short tale about a short Martian, from Alpha 7's card back. *Courtesy of Timmy's Toy Dungeon, Inc.*

Commander Comet is $60-70 loose, $600-700 carded. *Courtesy of Timmy's Toy Dungeon, Inc.*

The Comet's tale, from his card back. *Courtesy of Timmy's Toy Dungeon, Inc.*

Colossus Rex is $80-90 loose, $800-900 carded. *Courtesy of Timmy's Toy Dungeon, Inc.*

A colossal explanation from his card back. *Courtesy of Timmy's Toy Dungeon, Inc.*

The back of Rex' card shows all seven characters, including the devilish Xodiac, who is $70-80 loose and $600-700 carded. *Courtesy of Timmy's Toy Dungeon, Inc.*

Here's Xodiac, in used condition, without his helmet or staff, so let's rate him at $40-45. *Courtesy of Paul Levitt.*

Here's Alpha 7 loose, with his helmet but no weapon. Let's give him, oh say, $60-70. *Courtesy of Paul Levitt.*

Orbitron loose, no accessories, in pretty good shape. Let's say $50-60. *Courtesy of Paul Levitt.*

Here's the 1970s Space Warriors Colorforms giant set, which includes Commander Comet, Alpha 7, Astro-Nautilus, and...

... Metamorpho, The Man From Alpha Centauri (with changeable faces) and Inferno, the Flame Man of Mercury...

... Cyclops, The Giant From Beyond the Milky Way...

... Gemini, the Man from the Twin Star Algol, Mysteron, the Man from Hollow Earth, and Gamma X, The Man From The Fourth Dimension, who glows in the dark. *Courtesy of Timmy's Toy Dungeon, Inc.*

Here's the interior of the play set.

... Inferno...

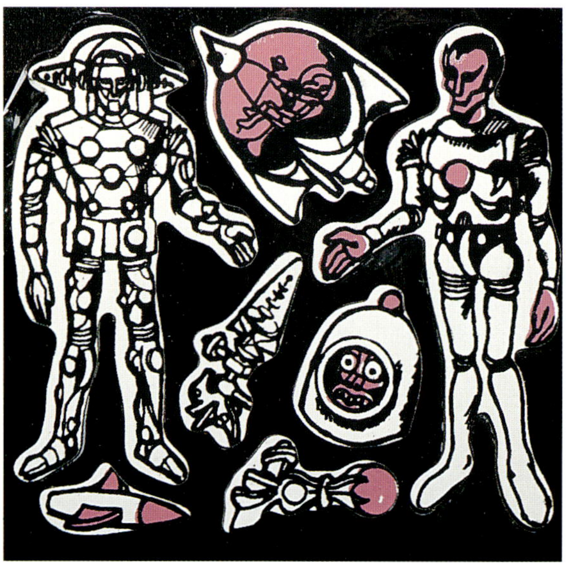

Here are Gamma X and Metamorpho,
a crucial element, man.

... Mysteron...

Commander Comet and Gemini...

... Cyclops and Astro-Nautilus...

... *and* Alpha 7. That's all nine characters depicted on the box lid. The only ones left out of this set were Electron +, Xodiac, Orbitron and Colossus Rex. *Courtesy of Timmy's Toy Dungeon, Inc.*

The designs for the Outer Space Men still pop up today. Check out these mini-figures from a 1990s generic space playset. $6-8 each. *Courtesy of Paul Levitt.*

A 1970s puzzle, with Xodiac (with helmet and staff), Colossus Rex and Astro-Nautilus. $40-50. *Courtesy of Paul Levitt.*

Here's more of 'em! *Courtesy of Paul Levitt.*

These 1990s monsters are kissin' cousins to the Outer Space Men, so we put 'em here. $5-6 each. *Courtesy of Paul Levitt.*

The Strange Change Machine, one of the all-time greats. You put some plastic squares in the transformation chamber and they grew into mini-monsters! Loose $40-50. Boxed $70-80. *Courtesy of Timmy's Toy Dungeon, Inc.*

This Membrane Man is a good example of the creatures you could make. *Courtesy of Timmy's Toy Dungeon, Inc.*

A typical Strange Change character. $5-6. *Courtesy of Timmy's Toy Dungeon, Inc.*

This zombie woman is one of many rubber creatures sold at dime stores in the 1960s and 1970s. She stands about 5" tall (well, sits) and is worth $15-20. *Courtesy of Play With This.*

Multiple Products issued a line of 6" plastic figures with removable, switchable heads called the Pop-Top Horrors. They generally run $15-20. Here's the Executioner. *Courtesy of Timmy's Toy Dungeon, Inc.*

With the Fright Factory, kids could make all sorts of squiggly jiggly stuff. $40-50. *Courtesy of Timmy's Toy Dungeon, Inc.*

This Motorized Monster Maker came equipped to create the large-toothed fellow to the left. That three-eyed Martian looks like the one from *The Angry Red Planet*. $50-60. *Courtesy of Play With This.*

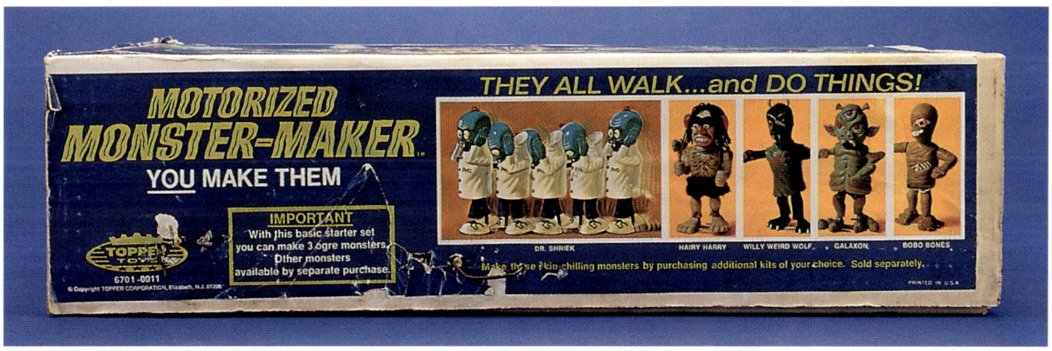

This box detail shows more of the creepies. Hey, I walk and do things too, but nobody ever made a toy out of me!

And this box detail shows the kit laid out. Easy, fun, and really weird, huh? Sounds like my last... *Courtesy of Play With This.*

Chompy the Beetle was one of many monstrous windups that populated the 1960s. $200-250. *Courtesy of Toyrareum Collectible Toys.*

This fellow is just the type of thing that I created this chapter to include. $30-40, whatever it is. *Courtesy of Paul Levitt.*

Krusher could be inflated using the valve on his belt. Then, you deflated him by CRUSHING HIM! GARR!!!!! You turkey necks! Loose $20-25. MIP $50-60. *Courtesy of Play With This.*

This crabentular citizen turns up in various playsets throughout the years, as figure molds get reused. This version is 6 inches tall! $3-4. *Courtesy of Paul Levitt.*

The Star Raiders was a line of 8" aliens created to cash in on the *Star Wars* craze. How, I'm not sure, but Tomland's line incorporated the four figures from Combex' Famous Monsters Of Legend (Fly, Yeti, Morlock, Cyclops) as well as eight new characters. Loose $30-40. MIP $70-80. *Courtesy of Timmy's Toy Dungeon, Inc.*

The back of the card shows 'em all, with names. The original four make up the left hand row. *Courtesy of Timmy's Toy Dungeon, Inc.*

"Man, that bus is late." *Courtesy of Paul Levitt.*

"Hello, Sailor!" *Courtesy of Paul Levitt.*

"How'd ya like DIS up dat skirt, nancy boy?" *Courtesy of Paul Levitt.*

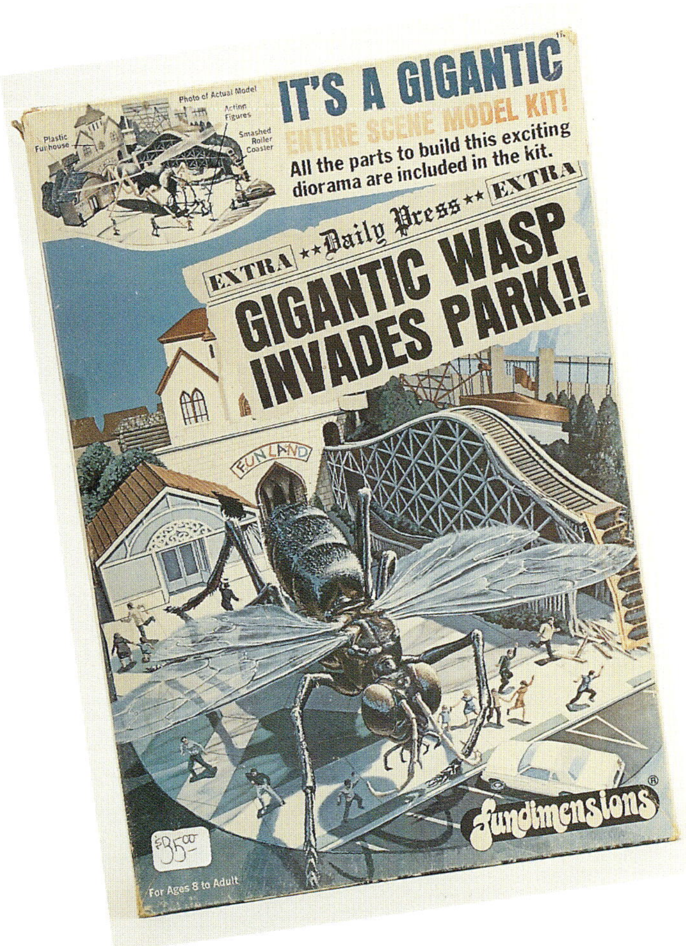

The Gigantics were four anatomically-correct insect models that came with miniature scenes and back-drops. They could be used as giant monsters or classroom exhibits, and how many toys can you say THAT about? $60-70. *Courtesy of Play With This.*

This side strip shows a kid trying to assemble the fragile background.

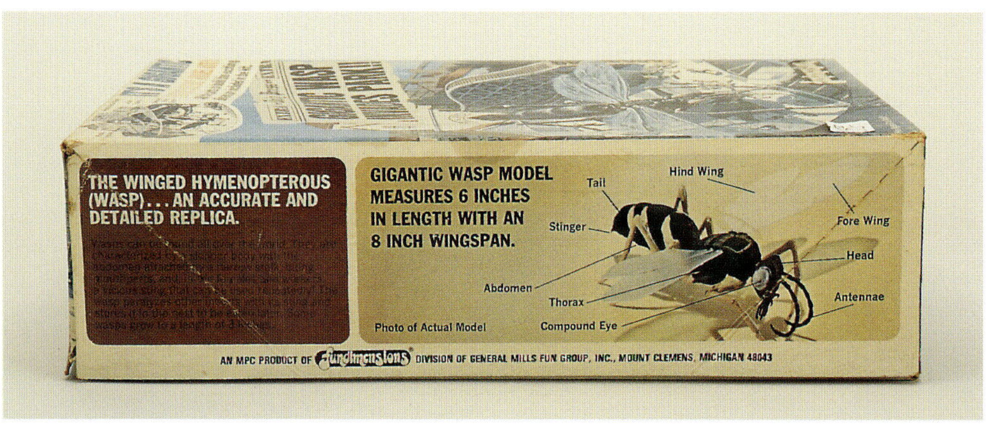

Here's the wasp. I could never get the wings to stay on mine. Maybe that's why it wasn't reissued in the 1990s with the Mantis, Scorpion, and Tarantula. *Courtesy of Play With This.*

The Inhumanoids were monsters created by Hasbro in the 1980s. Here's the leader, Metlar! $40-50 loose, $90-100 boxed. *Courtesy of Play With This.*

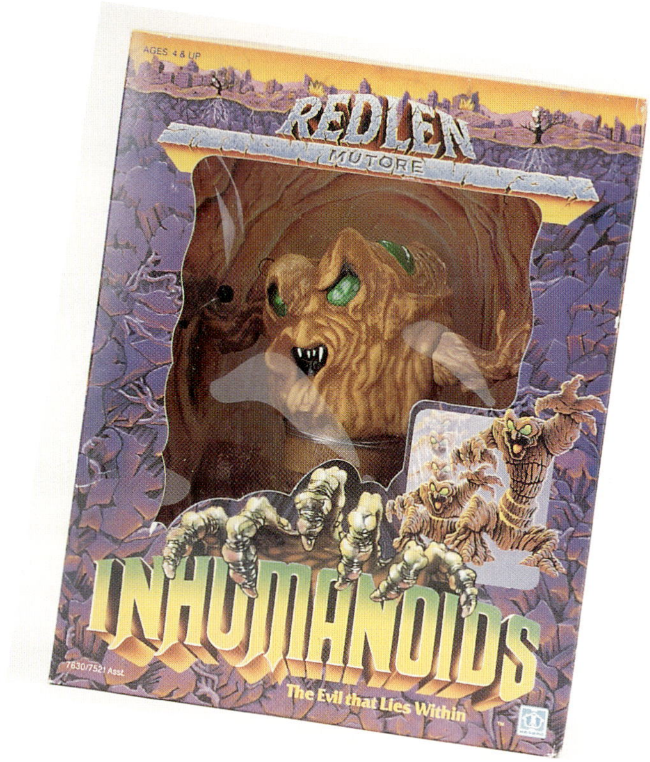

The Inhumaoids was a Hasbro line that never caught on, but I loved it. Redlen is $10-12 loose, $20-25 boxed. *Courtesy of Toyrareum Collectible Toys.*

The box back shows the world of the Inhumanoids. You start at the Earth's crust and then you keep going down and down and down...

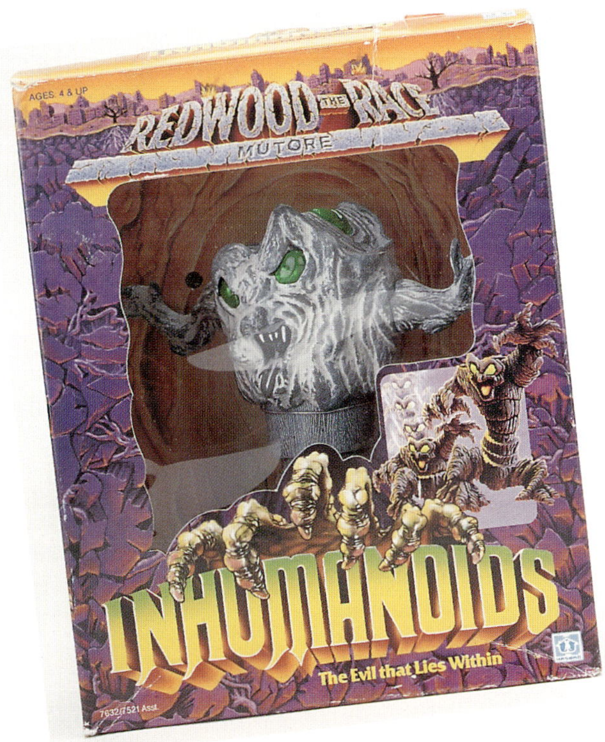

This Redwood is one of Redlen's underlings. They had an uneasy alliance with Mankind against the main villains. *Courtesy of Toyrareum Collectible Toys.*

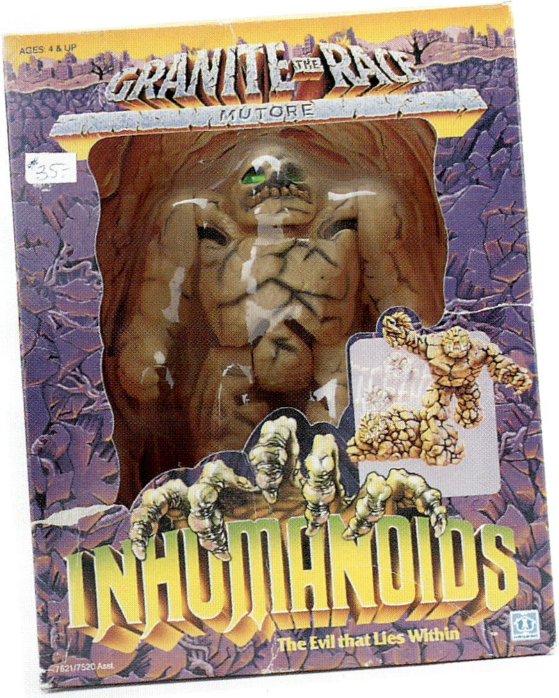

The Granites also could never make up their minds about whose side they were on. Loose $10-12. MIP $30-40. *Courtesy of Toyrareum Collectible Toys.*

Magnokor, leader of the Granites, could split in two. Loose $12-15. Boxed $30-40. *Courtesy of Paul Levitt.*

The fantasy phase in the early 1980s gave us great generic monsters like this dragon lizard. $4-5. *Courtesy of Paul Levitt.*

Here they are O.O.P. (out of package). *Courtesy of Paul Levitt.*

One of the least-known figure lines of the 1980s was The Other World, a series of bendable characters and monsters who lived in a Conan-esque fantasy setting. Here's a wolf beast from the line, $6-7. *Courtesy of Play With This.*

More Other World residents. $6-7 as shown. *Courtesy of Play With This.*

This tatzelwurm is actually a bracelet when you flip the tail up. $4-5. *Courtesy of Paul Levitt.*

And here's a member of the 1980s Monster Man line, a "me too" line from Woolworth's, designed to play with He-Man. Loose $3-4. MIP $10-12. *Courtesy of Nick Delliponti.*

Rocks N Bugs N Things was a line of creatures that disguised themselves as rocks to catch the plastic bugs they ate by surprise. (!!!!!) Loose $3-4. MIP $8-10. *Courtesy of Play With This.*

Here are two more of the "rocks." Hey, that's the 1980s for ya! *Courtesy of Play With This.*

This three headed Chimera can count snake, lion, and goat among its contributors. Goat Head?!? BURN THIS EVIL BOOK!!!! Loose $5-6, MIP $15-20. *Courtesy of Paul Levitt.*

Advanced Dungeons and Dragons had an extensive figure line that included proper action figures as well as plastic statuette figures, like this Shambling Mound. Loose $2-3. MIP $15-18. *Courtesy of Play With This.*

This Fire Elemental is another statuey type. Loose $4-5. MIP $12-15. *Courtesy of Play With This.*

This Raging Roper (oh, Stanley!) was a bendy monster ALSO from Advanced D&D. Loose $5-6, MIP $15-18. *Courtesy of Play With This.*

Another fantasy action figure line, Blackstar, offered these demon "familiars" with its bad guys. $2-3. *Courtesy of Nick Delliponti.*

This cool chap is a He-Man knockoff from the 1980s that looks better than most real He-Man monsters. Loose $2-3. MIP $8-10. *Courtesy of Nick Delliponti.*

During a more innocent time, the late 1970s, Bigfoot was presented as a lovable monster. Game $20-25. *Courtesy of Play With This.*

The game board led you around to deposit footprints.

Monsters of all kinds turned up as toys in the 1980s. Here's a dragon Flash something. Loose $2-3. MIP $7-8. *Courtesy of Timmy's Toy Dungeon, Inc.*

The plastic Bigfoot figurine on the left deposited "foot-print" pogs on the game board when you pressed down on it. Making a farting sound while doing so was mandatory.

Left:
We don't know when these gumball machine guys were made, or anything else about them, but they're cool monsters, so here they are. $4-5 each. *Courtesy of Timmy's Toy Dungeon, Inc.*

Right:
Rampaging Robot bendy from Just Toys. 1990s. $5-6. *Courtesy of Paul Levitt.*

Parents of the 1990s had a field day boycotting Rude Ralph, who made random disgusting noises when you pulled his eye out. $20-30. *Courtesy of Rude Paul Levitt.*

Editor Jeff Snyder said, "If you're doing a monster toys book, you've GOT to have an Aurora Guillotine it in it." So here it is, although it isn't a monster. The guy who invented the Guillotine wound up in one. Built Up $50-60. Boxed $200-250. With Madame Tussaud's logo on the box, $300-400. *Courtesy of Toyrareum Collectible Toys.*

Paul Levitt was so thrilled when he found this google-eyed, flailing dinobeast that he called me immediately to tell me about it. "Moo! Moo! Moo!" says the Dinobeast. $3-4. *Courtesy of Paul Levitt.*

On the subject of Aurora, here's the Glow version of the Witch, $200-250 boxed. *Courtesy of Toyrareum Collectible Toys.*

And on the subject of witches, here's an MPC plastic figure approximately 3" tall, 1960s. $20-25. *Courtesy of Timmy's Toy Dungeon, Inc.*

Below:
Still in the 1960s, here's this fellow, who has been issued repeatedly over the years for the use of stressed out squeezaholics. This is the 1990s version.

Here's the Witch, built up, $30-40. Rat tails intact! *Courtesy of Toyrareum Collectible Toys.*

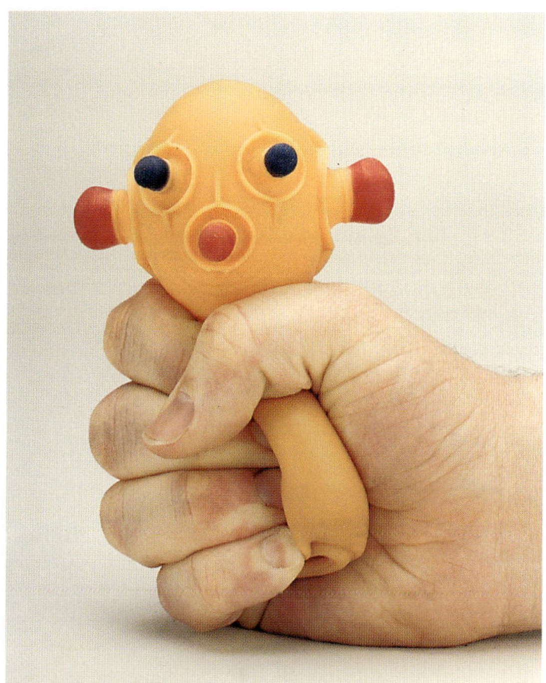

SQUEEEEEEEEEEEZE!!!!!!
$10-12. *Courtesy of Jeffrey "Squeeze" Snyder.*

This may look like a lunch box but it's a carry case for 1990s Monster Women! $15-20. *Courtesy of Timmy's Toy Dungeon, Inc.*

The flip side shows some of the Monster Women in question. *Courtesy of Timmy's Toy Dungeon, Inc.*

Scorpion Monster Woman, $2-$3.

And a Tarantula Monster Woman. $2-3.

And a centipede Monster Woman! $2-3.

And a Bat Monster Woman! $2-3.

And a— uhh— a finger puppet that came in the Monster Women lunch pail! $2-3. *All Courtesy of Timmy's Toy Dungeon, Inc.*

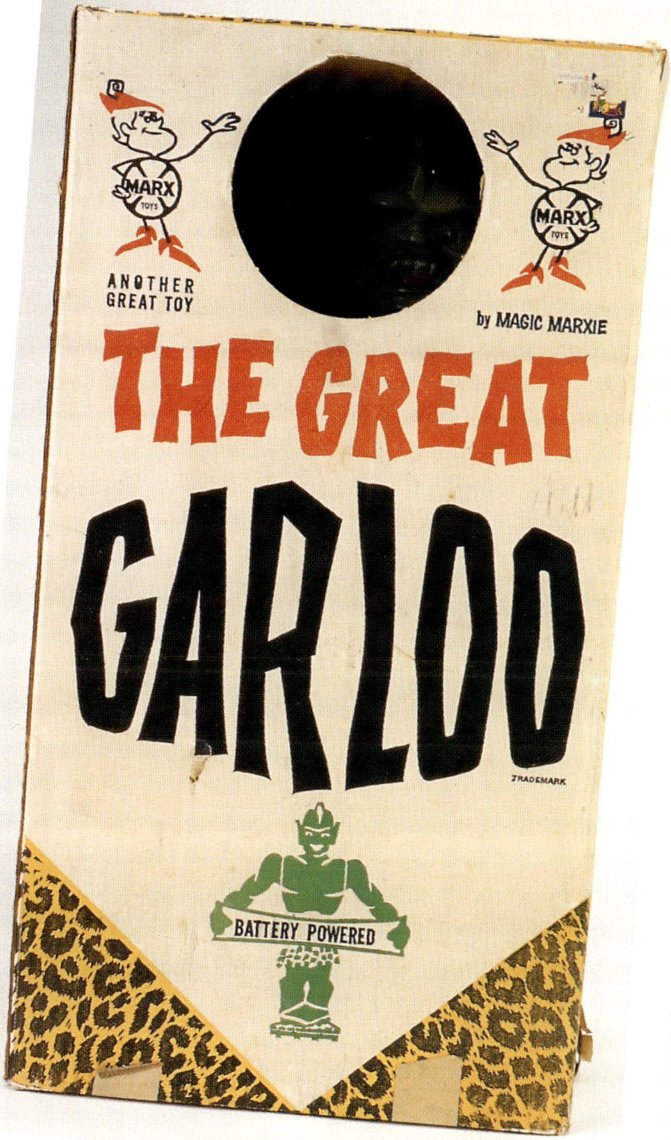

No book on Monster Toys could possibly exist without The Great Garloo by Marx. Loose $300-400. MIP $600-700. *Courtesy of Toyrareum Collectible Toys.*

The box lets you know who's boss.

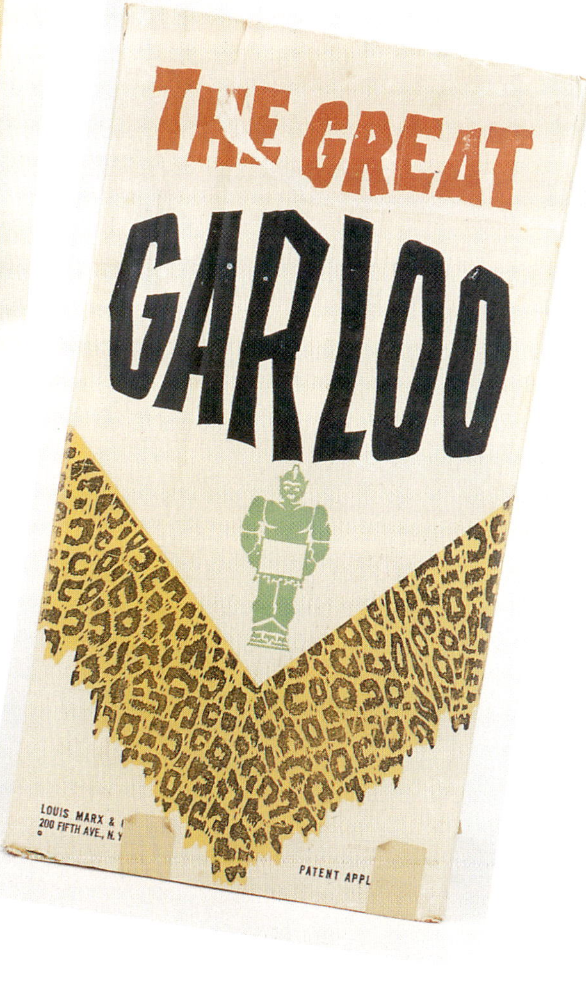

The back of the box let's you know who's inside.

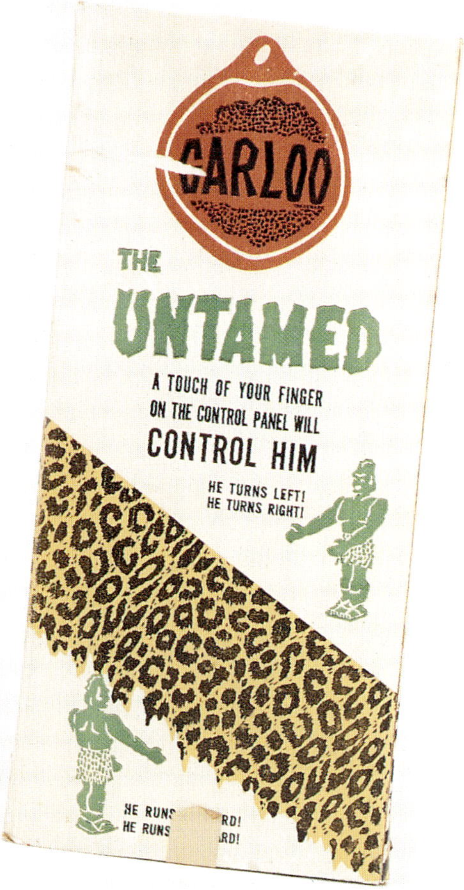

But beware! He's untamed!

Here he is!

His medallion boasts proudly who he is!

Think you can tame him?

But you can control him—with this! I like the steering wheel, nice touch.

He must be a she! Here's Junior! $300-400 as shown. *Courtesy of Toyrareum Collectible Toys.*

An illegitimate son! (No medallion!) *Courtesy of Toyrareum Collectible Toys.*

And leave us not forget that other 1960s monster icon, Horrible Hamilton and his insectoid invaders! Boxed set $800-900. *Courtesy of Toyrareum Collectible Toys.*

Chapter 6. MODERN MONSTERS

Starting with *Alien*, monster movies have become much more sophisticated in their storytelling techniques and content.

The typical monster character of the last two decades is an anti-hero, in spite of how many people it slaughters. The monster now more than ever gives a cathartic thrill to his audience. Thus, the new breed of monsters rates a chapter all its own.

The fact that monsters are becoming heroes has not been lost on the parents of America, who aren't happy about it. This began at the very start of the modern monster era. Kenner's launch of an 18" Alien was met with such resistance that the company canceled its proposed line of pocket-sized figures which was to include a Ripley and several other characters in addition to the Alien.

Of course times have changed, and Kenner did revive the Alien action figure concept with much success in the 1990s.

Freddy Krueger is another matter. Because of the stylized films in which he starred, Freddy has come across as more cool than cruel, more snazzy than scary, and so he too became the focus of merchandising aimed at kids. And it, too, suffered from parental complaints, which eventually drove Freddy merchandise off the market.

Other monsters of our modern age have had varying degrees of success, but one thing is certain: we have entered a brave and scary new world, in which what once was thought of as repulsive and evil is now seen as reactive and powerful.

As we head into the next millennium, maybe monsters aren't the thing we should be fearing. Maybe we should be fearing ourselves.

The granddaddy of all modern-era monsters, the Alien from- uhh... uhh... *Courtesy of Nick Delliponti.*

Here's his creepy carapace, always the first thing to break! *Courtesy of Play With This.*

Let's examine this specimen. Note the easily-lost upper back spine and the detailed glow in the dark face paint.

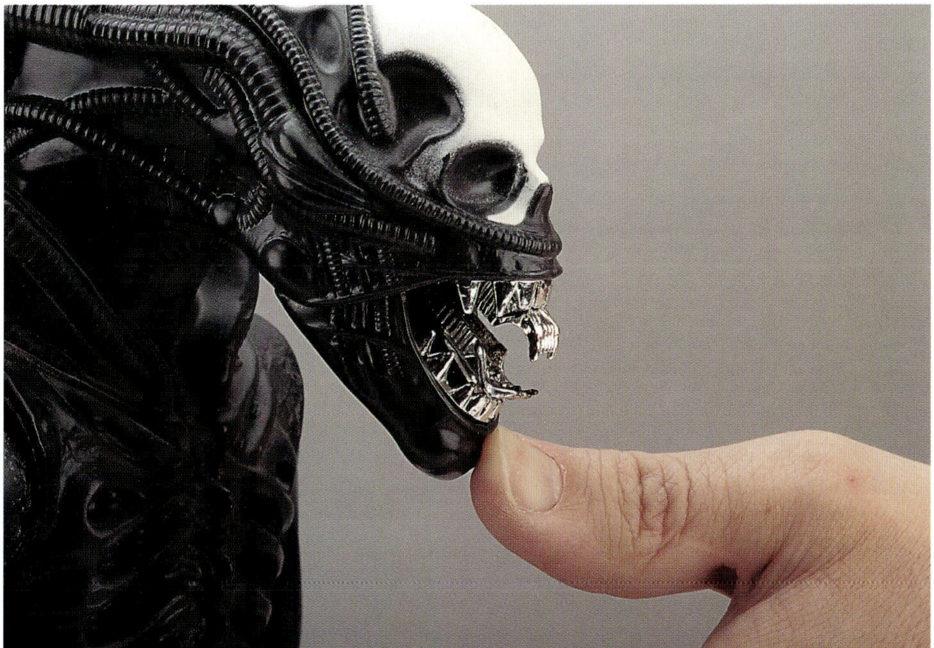

The inner mouth was advanced by opening the jaw. It had upper and lower clamps. Loose figure (with transparent dome) $200-250. Boxed $500-600. *Courtesy of Nick Delliponti.*

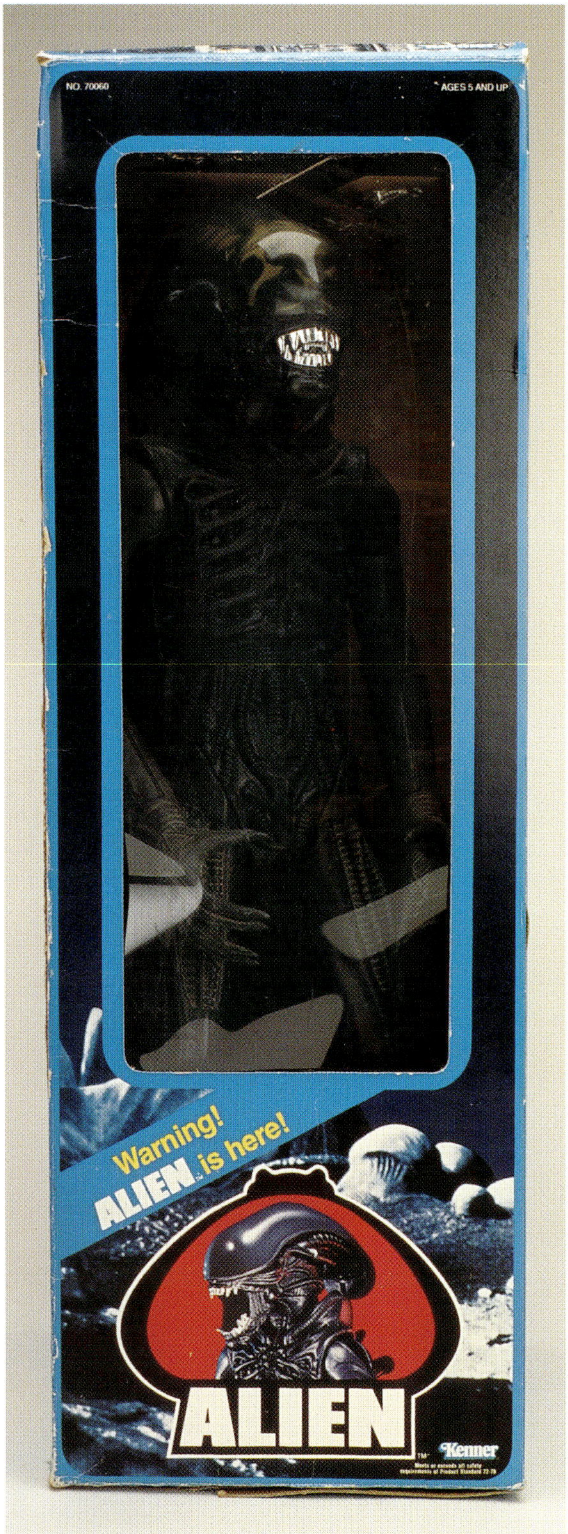

Here he is boxed. $500-600.
Courtesy of Play With This.

Side panel!

Another panel!

Yet another panel!

This fellow has been outfitted with a copy of his carapace. We couldn't find a black one, but Nick had a grey one which he hastily spray painted for us. *Courtesy of Nick Delliponti.*

Here's a vintage puzzle. $30-40. *Courtesy of Toyrareum Collectible Toys.*

Here's the Alien Game, decorated with what appears to be a painted-up Kenner Alien figure. *Courtesy of Play With This.*

A nice illo greeted you when you opened the box. *Courtesy of Play With This.*

And the game board wasn't bad, either. *Courtesy of Play With This.*

The playing pieces featured astronauts as well. The game runs $60-75. *Courtesy of Play With This.*

This Bop Bag is another example of 1990s *Alien* merchandise. $15-18. *Courtesy of Play With This.*

Face Hugger, same deal. Released at the time of *Alien Resurrection*. $30-40. *Courtesy of Paul Levitt.*

The movie *Aliens* was so successful that Kenner crafted toys for it in the 1990s, several years after it came out. The only proper 5" action figure they made was in the Aliens/ Predator two-pack. $6-8. *Courtesy of Nick Delliponti.*

A Baby Alien, yet more "dream" merchandise realized nearly 20 years later. $30-40. *Courtesy of Paul Levitt.*

A clock? Why not? $30-40. *Courtesy of Kollector's Choice.*

A cute little stuffed Gizmo. Awwwwwwww. $20-30. *Courtesy of (of all places) Timmy's Toy Dungeon, Inc.*

Gremlins had better luck than *Alien* in the merchandising department. Here's the giant 14" Gremlin. Loose $30-40. MIP $100-125. *Kourtesy of Kollector's Choice.*

Here's a 7" bendy Stripe. Loose $15-20. MIP $30-35. *Courtesy of Play With This.*

These PVC figures were based on *Gremlins 2*, which had Christopher Lee and not much else. $2-3. *Courtesy of Play With This.*

Same deal. *Courtesy of Play With This.*

Left:
Does two Gizmos beat a pair of Stripes? $15-20. *Courtesy of Play With This.*

This Marshmallow Man from *Ghostbusters* is almost impossible to find loose with all its paint. But for you, we found one, thanks to our lay-outer Blair. Loose $12-15. MIP $40-50. *Courtesy of Blair Loughrey*.

The "V" visitor was a hard-sell because it was the only 12" figure on the market at the time. Who's gonna fight him? Ken? I'd like to see that! Loose $12-15. MIP $25-30. *Courtesy of Play With This*.

Maxx FX was a great idea, a makeup man who dressed as various monsters. Planned releases included Frankenstein, Dracula, and the Alien, but parental anti-Freddy pressure shut the line down. Boxed $50-60. *Courtesy of Nick Delliponti*.

See how cool it was? Loose $15-20. *Courtesy of Nick Delliponti.*

This Freddy figure is squeezable and lovable—just like Freddy. $20-25. *Courtesy of Play With This.*

Parental pressure also saw a quick end to this game, in which players are "possessed" by Freddy. $40-50. *Courtesy of Nick Delliponti.*

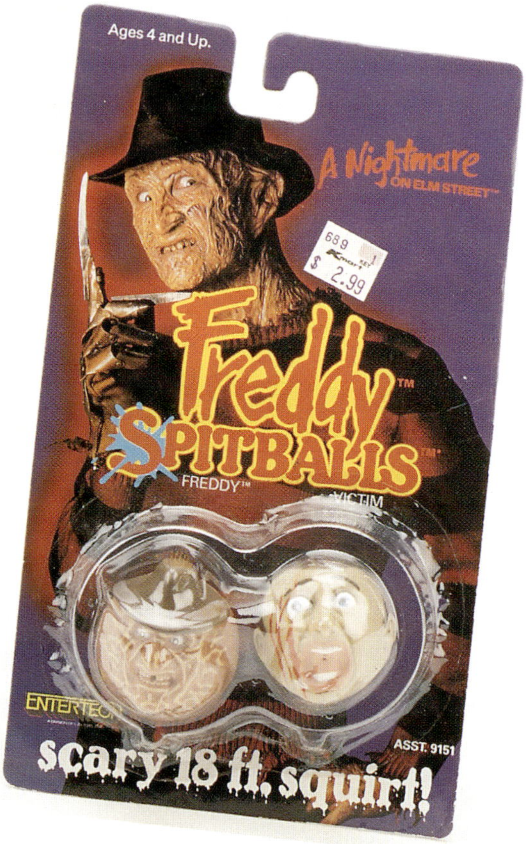

I love the faces on these Spitballs. $10-12 loose (pair). MIP $15-18. *Courtesy of Nick Delliponti.*

Another cute Freddy figure. Loose $10-12. MIP $20-25. *Courtesy of Play With This.*

Two Talking Freddies. Matchbox wimped out and took their logo off the package.

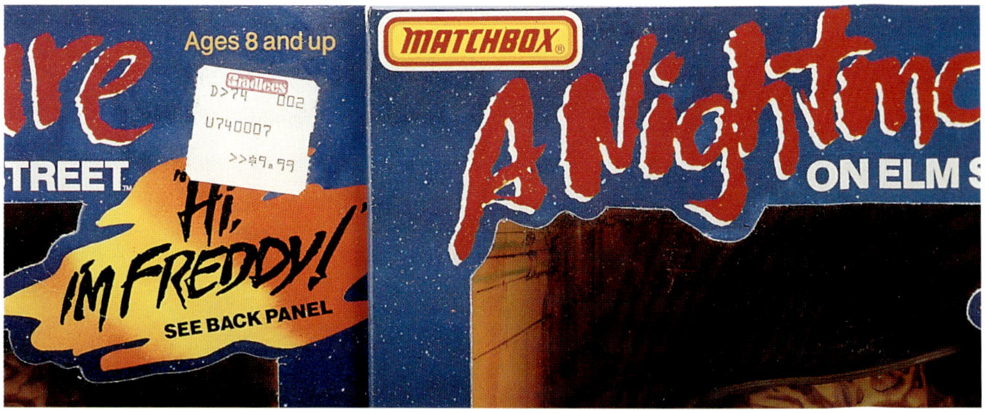

In this highlight you can see the Matchbox logo in the upper left of the box on the right, where the box on the left just had a blank space. Loose $20-25. No logo box $40-50. Logo box $60-70. *Courtesy of Nick Delliponti.*

He's getting the shock of his afterlife, kiddies! HeeeHeeHaHa *oh shut up already*. $25-30. *Courtesy of Nick Delliponti.*

This Freddy yo-yo had another great face. Loose $6-8. MIP $12-15. *Courtesy of Nick Delliponti.*

The Talking Crypt Keeper came in two version. One wears a Hawaiian shirt, and the other, by far the more distinguished, debonair, and sought after of the two, wears a tux. Loose $20-25. Boxed $30-40. *Courtesy of Play With This.*

The Crypt Keeper got his start in the 1950s, in comic books, but as always, it took mass media to make him a merchandising icon. $20-25. *Courtesy of Nick Delliponti.*

The Crypt Keeper strums us out of Monster Toys as one of the Dead Elvi. $4-5. *Courtesy of Sue Holmes.* Cowabunga, Begorah!

BIBLIOGRAPHY

Bonavita, John. *MEGO ACTION FIGURE TOYS*. Schiffer, 1996.

Cain, Dana. *COLLECTING MONSTERS OF FILM AND TV*. Krause, 1997.

Main, Jim (Editor). "Monster Collectibles Price Guide." *COLLECTIBLE TOYS AND VALUES* magazine #12, Attic Books, October 1992.

Main, Jim, and Erhard, Scott. "Moviemania: Collectibles from the Black Lagoon." *COLLECTIBLE TOYS AND VALUES* #42, Attic Books, March 1996.

Marshall, John. *G.I.JOE AND OTHER BACKYARD HEROES*. Schiffer Publishing, 1997.

Marshall, John. *ACTION FIGURES OF THE 1980s*. Schiffer Publishing, 1998.

Marshall, John. *ACTION FIGURES OF THE 1960s*. Schiffer Publishing, 1998.

McGonagle, John: "The Aurora Monster Scenes Kits." *COLLECTIBLE TOYS AND VALUES* magazine #10, Attic Books, July 1992.

Polizzi, Rick. *CLASSIC PLASTIC*. Collector Books, 1996.

Spears, Bruce. "Spectreman." *ACTION FIGURE NEWS* magazine #4, Lee Publications, Fall 1991.

Spears, Bruce. "The History of Godzilla Toys." *ACTION FIGURE NEWS* magazine #5, Lee Publications, Winter 1992.

Tumbusch, T.N. *TOMART'S ENCYCLOPEDIA AND PRICE GUIDE TO ACTION FIGURES*. Tomart Publications, 1996.

Van Plew, Mike. "Bionically Connected." *COLLECTING TOYS* magazine, Kalmbach Publishing, February 1997.